Governance of Federal Regulatory Agencies

Governance of Federal

Regulatory Agencies

by David M. Welborn

The University of Tennessee Press
Knoxville

Library of Congress Cataloging in Publication Data

Welborn, David M   1934–
  Governance of Federal regulatory agencies.

  Bibliography: p. 171
  Includes index.
  1. Independent regulatory commissions—United States.
I. Title
JK901.W4   353.09'1   77-8012
ISBN 0-87049-216-0

For my mother and father

Preface

In broadest terms, this book is an exploration into the politics within several institutions—independent regulatory agencies—concerned with control of economic activity at the national level. Although it is well understood that great power has gravitated to departments, agencies, bureaus, commissions, and other administrative bodies, our grasp of their inner life is limited. Studies in settings such as legislative halls, courts of chief executives, and even judicial conference rooms clearly demonstrate the importance of relationships and processes which constitute institutional fabrics for the decisions which are made, in conjunction with the large political forces which play on decision centers. In recent years there has been increasing research attention given to decision-making within departments and agencies and the relationship between institutional characteristics and policy results. But much remains unilluminated, in comparison with what is known about Congress and even the White House, for example. It is hoped that this analysis will add to a growing understanding of politics in administrative settings, in addition to revealing something about the inner life of several governmental institutions which are important in their own right.

The book is a revision of a study prepared under the auspices of the Administrative Conference of the United States. The conference deserves credit for whatever of value may be found here and none of the blame for errors. The findings and views expressed are only mine and have not been approved or endorsed by the conference.

A large number of persons contributed to the study in important ways, and to them I extend my great appreciation. Dean Roger Cramton of the Cornell University School of Law was the guiding spirit and prime mover in its initiation when chairman of the conference. Professor Norman Thomas of the University of Cincinnati also played an important role at the beginning stage. The execution of the study was facilitated by subsequent chairmen of the conference, Antonin Scalia and Robert Anthony. Throughout, several members of the conference staff provided assistance and encouragement, particularly Richard Berg, Jo Carter, John Cushman, and Ruth Hartman. The study was guided by the conference's Committee on Agency Organization and Personnel. Max Paglin, chairman of the committee, was a constant help through his understanding of the questions under examination and appreciation of the importance of exploring them. Earl Kintner, a former regulatory commission chairman, also supplied enthusiastic support and assistance. Other members of the committee regularly reviewed materials and reacted in helpful ways. They were: Carl A. Auerbach, Charles F. Bingman, Warren E. Blair, Paul G. Dembling, Ronald M. Diertrich, Robert G. Dixon, Jr., Stanley Ebner, Anthony L. Mondello, William A. Nelson, John H. Powell, Jr., Ashley Sellers, Meade Whitaker, and Joseph Zwerdling.

Seventy persons kindly set aside time for what in many instances were long conversations about regulatory processes and their candid perceptions of them. These interviews are the raw materials for the analysis, and without them there could have been no study. My colleagues, Paul Schulman and Dan Nimmo of the University of Tennessee-Knoxville and Emmette S. Redford of the University of Texas-Austin, read the manuscript and made helpful suggestions. Ann Thompson and Mark Wattier provided research assistance. Teresa Bradley, Estella Armstrong, Irene Fansler, and especially Martha Evers saw much more of confused drafts than they would have wished for but managed to translate those pages into decent manuscript form with astounding tolerance and good humor. Aline and Amy were patient, and after three years will be more thankful than anyone that there is now a conclusion.

DAVID M. WELBORN

Knoxville, Tennessee
October 1, 1976

Contents

Tables

Figure

Governance of Federal Regulatory Agencies

1.

Introduction

Small groups of public officials—among whom are the several members, chairmen, and from time to time key staff members of the
various regulatory commissions—meet frequently in conference
rooms scattered about Washington, D.C., to make decisions based
upon broad discretionary authority conferred by Congress. The
decisions of these officials shape economic activity in the nation in
important ways: Prices of basic commodities and services, such as
energy, transportation, and communications, are affected; and the
structure and practices of important industrial sectors are influenced
by the policy statements, rules, and orders which are forthcoming.
Collectively, as the designated leaders of the commissions, the members and chairmen function as major instruments with which the
national government exercises substantial power over the economy.

Seven regulatory commissions—the Civil Aeronautics Board, the
Federal Communications Commission, the Federal Maritime Commission, the Federal Power Commission, the Federal Trade Commission, the Interstate Commerce Commission, and the Securities and
Exchange Commission—are the subjects of the analysis to follow.
Other commissions are engaged in the regulation of economic
activity, including long-established agencies, such as the Federal
Reserve Board and the National Labor Relations Board, and some
of recent creation, such as the Commodity Futures Trading Commission, the Consumer Product Safety Commission, and the Nuclear
Regulatory Commission. A large number of regulatory programs are
carried out by still other agencies lacking commission features, such
as the Food and Drug Administration in the Department of Health,
Education and Welfare and the Environmental Protection Agency.
But the "Big Seven," as they are often characterized, have a special

prominence in economic regulation because of their established nature, the importance of the functions they perform, and the political controversies which often surround them.

Each of the seven agencies is engaged in complex regulatory and, in some instances, promotional tasks. Five are involved continuingly and pervasively in particular industrial sectors. They regulate entry, prices, financial arrangements and control, business conduct, and competitive practices. The Civil Aeronautics Board has jurisdiction over civil air transportation; the Federal Communications Commission exercises control over common carriers employing wire or the radio spectrum; the Federal Maritime Commission regulates shipping in offshore commerce; the Federal Power Commission is concerned with hydroelectric power and natural gas; and the Interstate Commerce Commission oversees various forms of surface transportation. Some of these agencies have other regulatory responsibilities of a more restricted character. The most important examples are the Civil Aeronautics Board's limited role in international and foreign air transport and the Federal Communications Commission's responsibilities for licensing and setting operating rules for users of the radio spectrum. The two remaining agencies, the Federal Trade Commission and the Securities and Exchange Commission, have roles of a different sort. The Federal Trade Commission's jurisdiction includes the economy as a whole in regard to corporate structure and competitive practices. In addition it provides particular protection for consumers in such things as textile and fur labeling, flammable fabrics, and credit practices. The Securities and Exchange Commission regulates facets of the securities industry's operations in order to protect investors, principally through the mechanism of disclosure.

The major focus of analysis is on the governance of the seven agencies, or their internal direction and control. Put in the simplest form, the central analytical problem is, within these organizations, who may be said to regulate and on what basis? What are the relevant capacities and effects of chairmen, commissioners, and staff; and how do they interact in processes leading to critical regulatory determinations?

Questions of agency governance may be addressed in any organizational context, but they are particularly intriguing in that type of agency represented by regulatory commissions. The commissions play a central role in the nation's economy. Economic conditions in the mid-1970s, a period marked by serious inflation, shortages in critical areas, such as energy, and other dilemmas, accentuate the importance of their performance, anatomy, and processes. But the organizational form they represent is inadequately understood. The formal arrangements set out in the relevant statutes cloud rather than reveal patterns of governance. At the top levels of these agencies, authority for overall direction and control is diffused among a group rather than placed in a single official. Although some differences are specified in the prerogatives of chairmen and the membership, ultimate formal responsibility for regulatory policy development and implementation is vested in eleven members of the Interstate Commerce Commission, seven members of the Federal Communications Commission, and five members of the remaining agencies, to be exercised in a collegial, shared manner. Thus in contrast with most public agencies in the United States that are headed by single executives, in these the formal executive structure is plural in character. Executive authority and the executive role are shared, supposedly, among the members of a group. Public organizations of this type, though very much in the minority, are not uncommon and certainly not unimportant. The regulatory agencies under examination here are the most conspicuous examples, but others dot the landscape at all levels of government, engaged in the regulation of economic activity as well as in other governmental undertakings. We possess only a limited understanding of the administration of government programs when executive responsibility is placed in boards or commissions rather than in a single official. An analysis of agency governance in these seven agencies should go at least part way in remedying the condition. Finally, over the years, agency governance has persisted as a significant problem in public policy regarding regulatory commissions and their performance. Many, including students of the regulatory process, former regulators, and those involved in assessments of governmental organization, have suggested and continue to suggest reorganization to excise commission arrangements as a means for improving performance.

Organization for Economic Regulation as a Public Policy Problem

The major policy controversies in economic regulation have concerned, historically, the extent and nature of governmental intervention into the economy and the quality of performance of governmental agencies in the execution of regulatory responsibilities. In the 1970s, both the extent of intervention and the quality of regulatory performance emerged again as major domestic policy concerns. A Republican administration initiated efforts to roll regulation back in certain areas, buttressed by a host of economists arguing that economic inefficiency has been a major consequence of excessive governmental control.[1] The President's Advisory Council on Government Organization, reporting in 1971, found extensive performance deficiencies in the regulatory commissions and recommended major organizational changes. Its report received considerable attention and contributed to a renewed interest in regulatory issues.

In its critical assessment, the council, headed by Roy Ash and generally called the Ash council, reiterates a familiar theme regarding regulatory commissions and their performance. Ineffectiveness stems from certain of their organizational characteristics. The first is "independence" of presidential authority and a consequent divorcement from the executive branch. The second is their collegial character.

Independence results from political considerations and provisions for the appointment and retention of commission members. The major political consideration is the assertion of independence, in particular by members of Congress and to an extent by the agencies themselves and interests affected by their work. The rationale supporting the assertion is that the commissions perform a unique combination of functions, including those of a legislative and judicial as well as an executive type. The constitutional principle of separation of powers requires that legislative- and judicial-type functions be insulated from presidential control. Furthermore, since most of the important activities of the commissions involve rate-making, licensing, and the promulgation of rules governing business practices—all traditional legislative functions—they are congressional surrogates in the main, and hence "arms" of Congress rather than instruments of the executive.[2] The rationale is not without its weaknesses. But problems in the argument do not dilute its persuasiveness, especially for members of Congress, or its practical effects.[3]

Members of all seven agencies are appointed by the president and confirmed by the Senate, and no more than a simple majority of members in each agency may be members of the same political party.[4] Appointments are made for fixed, staggered terms ranging from five to seven years, depending on the commission. The question of removal is a complex one, but in general a president may not remove a member as easily as he makes changes among top-level officials in departments and agencies headed by single administrators. In some commissions it is clear that removal can come only for cause. In others the legal situation is clouded, but the political restraints have been sufficient to preclude presidential removal of members in either case.[5]

There is a thinness in the insulation from the presidency which the concept of independence and supporting arrangements provide. One factor is that resignations and deaths often allow more extensive opportunities to shape commission membership than a simple reading of the statutory provisions would indicate.[6] Another factor of significance is the chairmanship of the commissions. The president appoints a member to serve as chairman. Appointments do not require Senate confirmation. With the exceptions of the Civil Aeronautics Board and the Federal Power Commission, it is clear that chairmen serve as chairmen, but not as members, at the pleasure of the president. In the case of the Federal Power Commission, an argument can be made that once appointed as chairman, the incumbent serves until the conclusion of his term as a member, and in the case of the Civil Aeronautics Board, the chairman appears to have a fixed one-year term. Although the legal context may be different, presidents generally have been able to deal with the chairmanship in these two agencies on the same basis as the other commissions.[7]

Presidents and their agents may become involved in and substantially affect the work of the commissions through a variety of other means.[8] In reality, the independence of the agencies is circumscribed significantly and perhaps is no greater than that which is typical of similar agencies fully within the executive branch. Nevertheless, the formal arrangements which differentiate the commissions from other agencies in relation to the president remain a subject of contention.

Justifications for independence and plural structures for agency direction and control basically relate to attributes believed to be important in decision-making processes in economic regulation. Many continue to assert the superiority and desirability of group decision-making under conditions of relative independence as an alternative to dominance "by a single will."[9] Impartiality, offered as one important attribute, is enhanced, it is argued, by the dilution or preclusion of narrow political pressures through the commission arrangement. Continuity in policy and development of the expertise required for handling complex economic problems are facilitated by stability in membership made possible by reliance on a group appointed for definite, staggered terms and protected against removal from office. The quality of decisions is strengthened by the consideration of varied points of view. The development of sound public policy over time is served by the expression of minority views which decision by commission allows.

In one of the major assessments of the regulatory process, the First Hoover Commission's Committee on Independent Regulatory Commissions stated the justification for collective decisions in this way:

> A distinctive attribute of commission action is that it requires concurrence by a majority of members of equal standing after full discussion and deliberation. At its best, each decision reflects the combined judgment of the group after critical analysis of the relevant facts and divergent views. This provides both a barrier to arbitrary or capricious action and a source of decisions based on different points of view and experience.
>
> This process has definite advantages where the problems are complex,

where the relative weight of various factors affecting policy is not clear, and
where the range of choice is wide. A single official can consult his staff but
does not have to convince others to make his views or conclusions prevail.
The member of the commission must expose his reasons and judgments to
the critical scrutiny of his fellow members and must persuade them to his
point of view. He must analyze and understand the views of his colleagues if
only to refute them.[10]

Despite such defenses of collegial processes and accolades received by commissions for their work from time to time, perhaps to
a greater extent than other types of government agencies, their
labors have been surrounded by criticism of performance. In part
criticism reflects the contentious nature of responsibilities involving
antagonistic economic interests. Over the years, however, sober assessments of performance grounded in a sense of the broad national
purposes underlying a system of economic regulation have pointed
to a variety of problems that seem to cut across the commission
spectrum.[11] Some problems concern the substance of regulation. The
critical bill of particulars includes failure to consider all relevant
interests in decision-making and undue responsiveness to the interests
of the regulated, failure to contend adequately with changing economic and technological conditions, failure to develop and apply clear
and meaningful standards to guide decisions, and failure to link
activities of policy significance with other policy centers in government.

Another set of performance problems concerns the conduct of
agency operations. Again, there is a familiar bill of particulars which
includes: procedural laxity or stringency, depending upon the perspective of the critic; delay in arriving at decisions; overemphasis on
handling matters on a case-by-case basis, or adjudication, at the
expense of broader legislative-type approaches to policy development; leniency in the enforcement of rules and orders; failure to set
regulatory priorities and to plan regulatory programs; and failure to
coordinate activities with related activities in other departments,
agencies, and commissions.

Critical assessments generally emphasize one of three major
diagnostic lines in identifying the causes of performance deficiencies:
the statutory bases of regulation; the political environment which
surrounds regulatory activity; and the organizational arrangements
employed in the conduct of regulatory programs.

Some economists argue that various statute-mandated interventions into the marketplace unwisely diminish competition and cause
economic inefficiency. From this perspective, it is not so much the
way agencies carry out their missions which results in unsatisfactory
performance, it is the nature of the missions themselves.[12] Others

have suggested that the statutes which establish the framework for regulatory action do not provide the necessary means for achieving basic objectives. They are often laced with "inadequate, outmoded, or vague substantive policies" and imprecise standards.[13] Instruments such as sanctions needed to secure regulatory results are inadequate. Coordinated action is hampered by the segmented allocation of responsibility among several agencies, as in the transportation area. Agency performance, then, is often invested with the inadequacies of congressional enactments which regulators cannot overcome, despite the best intentions and concerted effort.[14]

The diagnostic line which emphasizes the political environments of the commissions and their impact on the behavior of regulators is suggested by Roger Noll. "Inherent in the regulatory process is a persistent tendency to make socially undesirable policy, even if the agency is motivated to "do good" rather than to promote the regulated industry."[15] The major political pressures on the commissions are exerted directly or indirectly by the regulated. Broader publics are concerned periodically rather than continually. As a result, regulatory agencies tend to be most responsive to the interests of the regulated, producing policies governing competition and prices that penalize the public-at-large in order to provide corporate satisfaction. In this perspective, responsiveness to the regulated does not result, basically, from the positive uses of corporate power to expropriate governmental authority as a simplistic captivity theory would suggest.[16] Responsiveness to the regulated flows from the limited presence of consumers in environments of the commissions. One consequence arises from a major motivation of the behavior of regulators: the desire not to be overruled in the courts or in Congress. A solicitousness results for potential challengers, particularly the regulated. Further, if a challenge is likely, commissions wish to avoid antagonists' claims of unfair treatment, reinforcing inclinations to take the positions of regulated interests into serious account. Responsiveness to the regulated is accentuated by the necessity to rely heavily on them for the information upon which decisions are based.[17]

The diagnostic line which emphasizes organizational characteristics as the source of performance problems has been the most important of the three, measured by official emphasis and efforts to bring about improvements. From this critical perspective, independence has a number of undesirable effects. It impedes development of coherent national policy in important economic areas. Commission divorcement from the broad streams of politics channeled through the presidential office causes a lack of responsiveness to changing conditions and popular views on economic questions, denial of broad public support for controversial steps which can be mobilized under presidential auspices, and a consequent accentuation of tendencies toward dependency on the regulated for political sustenance. Placing ultimate authority and responsibility in multi-membered bodies also results in "multiple direction" and "splintered management."[18] Deficiencies in substantive decisions and a host of operational difficulties have been associated with the perceived disarray in agency governance which is inevitable in the collegial form.[19]

Assessments emphasizing these themes have been widely debated as organization for economic regulation has emerged periodically as a public policy issue, with argument centering on the nature and implications of independence and the collegial arrangement. Resistance to major changes that would enlarge presidential authority over the commissions has been persistent and for the most part successful. At several points, however, congressional approval has been given to adaptations in formal arrangements for agency governance in the name of improved performance. The major ones have concerned the position of chairman and will be dealt with in some detail in chapter 2. Essentially, as a result of executive orders and legislation implemented in the 1950s and 1960s at the initiative of Presidents Truman and Kennedy, weight was added to chairmanships. The orders and legislation provided for presidential appointment and for extending the responsibilities of chairmen regarding personnel, budgeting, and other aspects of agency management. The adaptations were intended to enlarge the functions of chairmen in day-to-day operations and to add to their leadership capabilities without sacrificing the supposed advantages of group decision-making, diminishing the ultimate responsibility of the collegial body, or significantly lessening independence.

It has now been more than one decade since the bulk of the adaptations were made. The commissions remain subject to severe criticism for their performance, and organizational inadequacies still appear prominently in critical assessments, as in the Ash council report. Its critique deserves summary in some detail. The collegial form of organization is found to be "obsolete."[20] The "inherent deficiencies"[21] of the commissions are defined broadly and include insufficient accountability to either the president or Congress and a lack of responsiveness to "changes in industry structure, technology, economic trends, and public needs."[22] The remedies proposed for unsatisfactory performance include the replacement of several commissions with organizations headed by single administrators responsible to the president.[23]

The report selects four aspects of regulatory administration for particular emphasis: policy formulation, accountability, recruitment of officials, and management. It is asserted that in each area weaknesses arise from structure. Policies tend to be "narrow, after the fact, and at times inconsistent,"[24] because they are generally formulated in the context of the particular case. In turn, this situation exists because "coequal commissioners too often have difficulty agreeing on major policy statements or rules. They tend to avoid the difficult, preferring to wait for a suitable case . . . which will force the issue . . . ."[25] Accountability is limited because of "an inability to fix responsibility due to the inherent diffusion of authority among relatively anonymous coequal members."[26] There are problems in recruitment because of the barriers to finding "well-qualified men with executive ability who are willing to serve on a body of coequals which has management responsibilities."[27]

The critique of the agencies from a management perspective is a bit more detailed and specific. A broad notion of management is employed, essentially meaning the "management of resources in day-to-day operations"[28] pertaining to the implementation of policy. As Glen O. Robinson has observed, the concept incorporates both the performance of the administrative support functions, such as personnel and budgeting, and the feasibility of substantive policy matters.[29] In the Ash council's view, the management of the agencies remains a shared responsibility requiring collective decisions even on small matters, with highly unsatisfactory results. The council argued that:

> Collegial bodies are not an efficient form for managing operations. They fail as managers because of the ambiguity of direction inherent in the separate authority vested in each of the members. For precisely the same reason that collegial bodies are often effective for making broad policy, they are ineffective for the management of that policy.[30]

The position relies heavily for support on statements of administrative ineptitude drawn from the President's Committee on Administrative Management, the Attorney General's Committee on Administrative Procedure, and the First Hoover Commission and its task force report. But the real foundations are the assertions that the collegial form *inevitably* results in "court-like behavior, leading to an overjudicialization of agency process" and "an absence of authoritative and adaptable management able on its own to exercise each management function in such a way as to carry out broad policy."[31]

As to particulars, coordination with other agencies is "impeded, if not frustrated, by the requirement that a majority position be reached before a commission can participate on a cooperative basis with another agency."[32] Policy adaptability is impaired as a result of "the fact that collegial administration, relying on compromise and case-by-case policy formulation, tends toward continuity . . . of policy."[33] Agency resources may well suffer misallocation. "While a . . . chairman may have theoretical authority to direct staff activities, as a practical matter the staff will be inclined to respond to all commissioners."[34] The legalistic environment which characterizes these agencies results in a "passive, overly-judicial approach in regulation," and the case emphasis impedes the establishment of priorities in regulation.[35]

According to the council, the alterations that have been made over time in the position of the chairman have been inadequate to counter the fundamental dysfunctions of the collegial arrangement.

> These efforts for strengthening or modifying the collegial form, while improving the performance of the commissions, did not go far enough. Each represented an attempt to cure deficiencies while preserving the essence of collegial organization, but each was ultimately unsuccessful because the deficiencies and the essence are inseparable.[36]

Basically, then, it is argued that the plural executive arrangement as seen by the First Hoover Commission more than twenty years ago remains a characteristic condition. Agency governance has not changed and is similar from commission to commission.

The analysis and recommendations of the Ash council raise a series of questions made all the more intriguing by a failure to demonstrate their empirical basis.[37] Thus the council's assertion that the character of agency governance has not changed despite efforts to integrate a substantial measure of executive authority in the position of chairman serves more to sharpen curiosity than to satisfy it. The council's report also demonstrates the continuing existence of organization for economic regulation as a public-policy problem and the importance of questions about agency governance in the regulatory setting.

Central Questions

The central questions addressed in subsequent chapters arise from an interest in organization for economic regulation as a public-policy problem. The starting point is not the performance characteristics associated with arrangements for agency governance as might appear on the surface, that which is usually employed. Instead, it is in the nature of the arrangements as they are revealed through examining the performance of regulatory tasks.

One set of questions concerns the nature of the actual arrangements for directing and controlling regulatory processes. Are they in the disarray suggested by the Ash council? Have efforts to integrate authority in chairmanships for certain aspects of agency governance had no effect? If the Ash council's characterization is incorrect, what is agency governance like in the commissions?

By and large, these questions must be answered in terms of the places of agency chairmen and their colleagues in the regulatory process. The analytical heart of the matter, then, pertains to relative capacities and effects of these officials in agency direction and control in the performance of administrative functions, in general agency management, and in substantive regulatory decisions.

Another set of questions aims at explaining patterns of governance and why and how chairmen are more or less influential than their colleagues in the various areas in which important choices are made. What resources do chairmen and members have to influence agency activity? What are the constraints? How do sets of resources and constraints play against one another to produce certain results? To what extent is the distribution of influence in regulatory agency governance stabilized and institutionalized? What, in general, can be said as to the potency of the *positions* of chairman and member, as contrasted with the potency of individual incumbents?

A final set of questions deals with agency governance in policy terms, cued by the specific criticisms of the Ash council. To what extent does the commission form constrain policy and program coordination, adaptability, appropriate allocation of resources, and agency activism? What are the implications of patterns of governance for the concepts of collegiality and independence and for understanding and improving regulatory performance?

An additional preliminary step must be taken prior to piecing together answers to the foregoing questions: to set out in general terms the analytical perspectives employed in that process.

2.

Agency Governance in Analytical Perspective

There are two analytical focuses which may be employed in an examination of agency governance. The first involves exploration of governance in the context of the relevant "community." It is concerned with the ultimate sources of the values and objectives manifested in regulatory activity. Essentially the focus emphasizes the environment which surrounds regulatory agencies—constituencies, Congress, the president, and other parts of the executive branch, for example—and its play on them. Although the particulars of agency organization and other internal features may be considered in relation to environmental factors, interest in the politics of regulation in the largest sense diminishes the significance of such phenomena.[1]

The second analytical focus is on governance in the agency context. It is employed here so that issues discussed in the previous chapter concerning the internal direction and control of commissions may be addressed. This focus, it should be noted, also involves taking into account selected aspects of the regulatory environment as they touch upon the direction and control of regulatory activity by agency decision-makers.[2]

Agency Governance in Regulatory Context

In regulatory agency context, governance involves two major functions: decision-making pertaining to regulatory values and objectives, or in areas of critical choice, and management of the complexity that characterizes regulatory processes. From either community or agency perspective, the basic stakes in agency governance are the fundamental values to be reflected in regulation and the objectives to be sought. The precise concerns may differ from agency to agency, but the following itemization, adapted from Emmette S. Redford's discussion of belief patterns underlying regulatory systems, indicates the nature and range of the choices which are involved.

1. The sense of the needs and interests to be served through regulation and the balance to be struck among various relevant public and private interests.

2. The latitude to be allowed private sector decision-makers in economic choices.

3. The extent to which competition is to be restrained or enhanced.

4. The extent to which regulatory authority is to be extended into managerial decisions.

5. The comprehensiveness and intensity of the system of controls to be applied.

6. The nature of the processes to be employed in the application of agency authority, especially in regard to the balance struck between the use of formal procedures and adjudicatory style and more flexible, less formal processes, including negotiation.

7. The extent to which regulatory choices are to be informed by political considerations related to positions held by elements in the agency's environment, in contrast to more "objective" economic, legal, and other criteria.[3]

On these matters, agency decision-makers are constrained at any given point in time by determinations previously made and expressed in statutes, generally accepted interpretations and applications, and even in deeply rooted, institutionalized points of view implanted in the agencies. Despite constraints, there is extensive opportunity, even the necessity for, the exercise of discretion regarding values and objectives. Although critical choice may take the form of adaptation rather than radical revision, their consequences are extremely important. When the ebb and flow of regulatory policy is surveyed from agency to agency, a certain continuity is apparent, but major shifts in policy are apparent as well.[4]

Examination of the decisional activity of agencies shows that much has little or no important implications for adapting or shaping regulatory values and objectives. Much of the work involves the routine application of positions previously forged to particular situations. The small proportion of choices which are critical and thus important from the perspective of agency governance falls into two broad categories. One pertains to the substance of regulation and the other to means for the implementation of regulatory programs.

The critical substantive choices determine the regulatory agenda, working priorities, outcomes in specific issues of consequence, and the stylistic characteristics of agency activity. The decisions which result from formal proceedings constitute only the "tip of the iceberg."[5] Much more is involved.

Regulatory agendas consist of notions of major problems and the associated broad strategies which guide regulatory activity. They give tangible meaning to abstract and at times contradictory statutory mandates and indicate what an agency is essentially about at a particular point. Agencies are often forced to make problem-defining agenda choices with large consequences. The contextual uncertainties and the stakes were succinctly captured by Rush Moody, a member of the Federal Power Commission, in a congressional hearing concerned with natural gas problems: "Are we supposed to use rates to elicit supply, or to control producer profits? Because the two objectives do not necessarily coincide."[6] Agency resolutions may be ascertained. The Federal Communications Commission's attention in recent years to children's television programming, the Federal Power Commission's concern for the supply of natural gas in interstate markets, and the Securities and Exchange Commission's commitment to the concept of an integrated national securities market are recent examples of important regulatory agenda items.

Agendas tend to be crowded, if not clogged, and regulatory agencies have limited resources with which to work.[7] It is not possible to get at all major problems simultaneously. These conditions accentuate the importance of the working priorities, or the allocation of agency resources and efforts among problems. From the perspective of agency governance, the determination of working priorities stands out in importance. Priorities reflect refinements of the regulatory agenda and determine what actually will be done. The agenda items just mentioned are also examples of high priority items.

Substantive decisions of consequence may take a variety of forms. Actions coming as a result of formal proceedings concerning rates, licenses, and business practices, for example, are the most visible. Antecedent decisions to institute a course of action are also important, as in the case of a Federal Trade Commission proceeding against concentration in a particular industry.[8] Decisions of consequence may come in less formal packages, ranging from positions taken on legislation before Congress, to the use of adverse publicity as a sanction on undesirable behavior,[9] to generally defined stances on regulatory matters, such as the Civil Aeronautics Board's moratorium on new route approvals in the early 1970s.

A stylistic dimension of regulation is closely associated with agendas, working priorities, and decisions in specific substantive issues of consequence. Stylistic characteristics include the relative activism or passivism with which an agency executes its responsibilities and strategic orientation on, for example, the use of "jawboning" as an alternative to formal proceedings or education as a substitute for coercion in enforcement. Style colors substantive decision-making.

It melds with agendas and priorities in shaping judgments regarding problems to be attacked, the depth of intervention into economic activity, and the location of the boundaries of regulatory authority. Style also has independent effects acquired through providing cues that influence the behavior of those subject to regulatory authority.

The second general category of decisions involving regulatory values and objectives, hence agency governance, includes determinations which, though removed from substantive attention to questions about industry structure, financial practices, and the like, affects their definition and response to them. They shape institutional character, or the context in which important substantive choices are made. For some, administrative or management support functions—personnel, budgeting, and defining organizational structure and processes—constitute mundane areas of activity with minimal significance. This perspective underestimates their impact. Philip Selznick has emphasized the importance of such functions in the context of larger organizational concerns. "In organizations, 'dynamic adaption,'" or basic institutional change, "takes place in the shadowy area where administration and policy meet."[10] He continues, "We must take this, not in the obvious sense that administrative devices execute and form policy, but rather in the sense that organizational procedures profoundly influence the kinds of policy that can be made . . . ."[11] Support functions influence the kinds of policy that can be made in a variety of ways, especially through resource allocation and the recruitment and placement of personnel with particular skills and orientations. Organizational structure and processes affect the representation of values and objectives in agency decision-making. Organizational capacity to carry through with agendas and priorities is molded through choices made in these areas.

Decisions affecting institutional character often take simple form and are most meaningful in their cumulative effects. The contexts in which they are made are not marked by the economic, technological, legal, and political complexity which usually surrounds important substantive decisions.

The core of agency governance is in the decisions that are made. But the management of attendant complexity is a vital supplementary aspect. To a large extent, the management of complexity is concerned with the uncertainties and antagonism which surround regulatory efforts. The major functions involved in management in this sense pertain to the flow of information into, from, and within the agency and its processing; representation of the agency to other participants in regulatory processes; negotiation with and among antagonistic elements; and integrating and interpreting segmented agency activity in coherent policy and program terms.

There are several closely linked and complex features of the commissions' political environments which are especially significant for
agency governance: the commissions often are subject to conflicting
pressures on major issues; decision-making in key matters often involves cooperation and agreement with other parts of government;
and they are highly vulnerable in political, policy, and program
terms.[12]

Although the interests subject to the authority of a regulatory
agency may be in general agreement on the broad outlines of policy,
such as the desirable extent of competition, there may be important
differences on particular issues. For example, various modes of surface and air transportation contend for advantage before the Interstate Commerce Commission and the Civil Aeronautics Board. The
Federal Communications Commission is regularly engaged in issues
which place the American Telephone and Telegraph Company against
those who wish to compete with it in providing communications
services and in issues which set broadcasters against the emergent
community antenna television (CATV) industry. A large measure of
the Federal Trade Commission's work involves business interest
versus business interest. Increasingly the Securities and Exchange
Commission is engaged in problems which divide various components
of the financial community. The two agencies in which the level of
intra-jurisdictional conflict seems lowest are the Federal Maritime
Commission and the Federal Power Commission. In the case of the
former, although differences are not wholly absent, the sense of
community seems quite pronounced. In the case of the latter, the
two major regulated groups, the interstate hydroelectric power and
natural gas industries, have distinct, generally nonconflicting concerns.

More is involved in political complexity than intra-jurisdictional
differences, however. There are, in addition, the interests of those
affected by the behavior of regulated entities and which are in conflict among themselves at times. Traditionally, in certain areas of
regulation, such as transportation and communications, users have
been an important element in the political environment of various
commissions. Five of the agencies consistently make decisions with
highly visible and pointed effects on local communities and com
munity-based interests in matters such as transportation, broadcasting, and energy. These interests, especially as they are asserted
through Congress, are a significant presence in regulatory processes.
Broad consumer interests have become more vocal and powerful in
recent years through the consumer movement and its growing support in Congress.

The necessity to cooperate extensively with other parts of government in important areas of decision-making arises in numerous contexts. The significance of Congress for the agencies needs no elaboration. From time to time, problems are of presidential concern. All of the agencies must work with various parts of the executive branch and with one another, often on a continuing basis. Ministerial necessity involves the commissions with the Office of Management and Budget, the Civil Service Commission, the General Accounting Office (not, of course, part of the executive branch), and the Department of Justice in budgeting, legislative clearance, personnel, information gathering, and federal court proceedings. Overlapping jurisdiction is a factor in a number of instances, the most notable examples being the Federal Trade Commission and the Department of Justice. Related responsibilities account for an extensive range of relationships, at times marked by antagonism rather than cooperation. The Department of Transportation is important for the Interstate Commerce Commission and the Civil Aeronautics Board, as is the Office of Telecommunications Policy for the Federal Communications Commission. Most of the agencies from time to time deal with questions having international implications, bringing them into the orbit of the Department of State and other departments concerned with foreign commerce. Environmental and energy questions and economic stabilization efforts have thrust most commissions into relationships with agencies having unique responsibilities in these areas. Among the commissions themselves, the three transportation agencies are concerned with matters in common from time to time. The Federal Trade Commission and the Federal Communications Commission have jointly pursued interests in children's television in recent years.

Political vulnerability involves susceptibility to being blocked or impeded in policy and program pursuits as a result of opposition from without. There are several sources. The stakes are often high in regulatory decisions. Costs are imposed by most actions and by inaction as well. Those who are adversely affected frequently have the means to employ legislative, executive, and judicial routes to appeal or counter both regulatory initiatives and inertia.

A final major element of complexity concerns the conduct of agency activities. Major regulatory problems are obviously complex problems. Inherent complexity is exacerbated by limitations on time and resources. Furthermore, there is a segmented character to regulatory activity. Major problems are rarely dealt with once and for all time. They rarely present themselves for attention in neat packages. The responses they generate are rarely the responses of one set of decision-makers. Varying combinations of members and staff are involved at different points, with any given action dependent to an extent upon prior decisions and, by the same token, to be influential in subsequent determinations. When the larger political uncertainties are added to these elements, the complex world of the regulator begins to take form.

The Ash council suggested that a major problem of the commissions was a limited ability to deal with complexity. How well the commissions in fact have done so, though an important question, is not of central concern here. The question is the effect of complexity on systems of agency governance. The answer, to anticipate subsequent discussion, is that the effect is considerable.

Chairmen and Colleagues in Agency Governance: Formal Arrangements

In essence, the answer to the question, "Who governs in the agency context?" derives from ascertaining patterns in the involvement of agency officials in critical choices and the management of complexity, and their relative influence when there is joint involvement.[13] Judge Henry J. Friendly once likened the regulatory process to the Serbonian Bog, "where armies whole have sunk," suggesting the hazards of explorations.[14] Efforts to specify the involvement and influence of chairmen, members, and staff of regulatory commissions must be tempered by an appreciation of the difficulties and subtleties involved and the likelihood of being able to apprehend patterns in only crude and approximate form.

The task is facilitated somewhat by concentrating upon the upper official echelons, and especially on chairmen and commissioners. This is not to deny organizational pluralism, diversity in the sources of important decisions, and the influence of those in the middle and lower reaches of the commissions. Essentially, however, decision-making in the agencies under examination appears to be relatively centralized. Capacity for definitive, independent action at lower levels on critical matters is limited. There is operative a general organizational dynamic suggested by Chester I. Barnard of delegation "up the line" of "responsibility for abstract, generalizing, prospective, long-run decision," a characterization very close to the meaning of critical decisions.[15] Through whatever mechanism, responsibility for decisions moves to upper organizational levels, and notwithstanding preparatory work below, there remains the special importance of "last contributions."[16] Observation also suggests that questions regarding regulatory values and objectives are the object of conscious, purposive attention at upper levels in commissions. In contrast, at lower levels such questions ordinarily are submerged in the application of perceived agency positions to particular situations. Politics among upper level officials tends to be about agency governance to a significant extent, and it involves the development, mobilization, and application of resources to achieve preferred results in the exercise of discretionary authority, especially in matters of broad policy and program significance.

An obvious starting point for ascertaining patterns of governance is the allocations of authority and responsibility found in statutes, formal agency elaborations, and organizational structure. They provide an initial characterization of agency governance based upon surface appearances, and they indicate subsequent lines of analysis.

Generally, the formal charters are clear, implicitly if not explicitly, that in substantive matters of consequence, ultimate authority and responsibility rest in the commissions. There are ambiguities, more pronounced in some cases than others, concerning the roles of chairmen and their colleagues in setting agendas and priorities and in external relationships. There is lesser ambiguity in delineations of authority and responsibility in determinations associated with "institutional character."

A bit of background regarding the nature of formal charters would be useful prior to delving into particulars. The statutory bases for the position of chairman in the Civil Aeronautics Board, the Federal Power Commission, the Federal Trade Commission, the Interstate Commerce Commission, and the Securities and Exchange Commission are quite similar. They were set in reorganization plans approved for the Interstate Commerce Commission in 1969 and had been set during the early 1950s for the others. Provisions regarding the chairmanship in the Federal Communications Commission and the Federal Maritime Commission are found in the relevant organic acts passed in 1934 and 1963. There has been elaboration through formal action at the agency level, except for the Securities and Exchange Commission. The elaborations vary considerably in specificity and importance. To a large extent they reiterate statutory language.

Care must be taken to avoid reading too much into vague phrases. Nevertheless, there are comparisons of interest to note.[17] The first concerns the general characterization of the chairman's role in relation to his colleagues. In formal terms, that role is differentiated from others in that the chairman functions as a surrogate for the commission regarding "executive and administrative functions" in the Civil Aeronautics Board, Federal Power Commission, and Securities and Exchange Commission. There is a different indication in the other agencies. The Federal Trade Commission and the Interstate Commerce Commission have gone beyond the surrogate concept, perhaps unintentionally, to confer general executive responsibilities on the position through characterizing the chairman as the executive head of the agency. Indeed, the Interstate Commerce Commission has gone even further and spelled out derivatives in authority and responsibility. In that agency, the executive mandate includes:

> (1) the over-all management and functioning of the Commission, (2) the formulation of plans and policies designed to increase the effectiveness of the Commission . . . , (3) prompt identification and early resolution, at the appropriate level, of major substantive regulatory problems, and (4) the development and improvement of staff support to carry out the duties and functions of the Commission.

The statutes concerning the Federal Communications Commission and the Federal Maritime Commission similarly designate the chairmen of those agencies, respectively, as the "executive head" and "chief executive and administrative officer."

Another point of comparison concerns arrangements for administrative support functions. The roles of chairmen and their colleagues generally are distinguished to a degree. With the exception of the Federal Communications Commission, to be examined as a special case later, chairmen are given responsibilities over the budget and personnel functions and the assignment of duties and responsibilities at the staff level. Chairmen of the Civil Aeronautics Board, the Federal Trade Commission, and the Securities and Exchange Commission, in addition, have been empowered since the 1961–62 period to assign responsibility within the agencies for the execution of delegated authority. In all cases, chairmen, in carrying out their functions, are to be governed by commission policy and by relevant "regulatory decisions, findings and determinations." In the Civil Aeronautics Board, Federal Power Commission, Federal Trade Commission, Interstate Commerce Commission, and Securities and Exchange Commission, the appointment of "heads of major administrative units" is subject to commission approval. Only in the Federal Power Commission and the Federal Trade Commission have there been formal identifications of these positions through commission action. The chairman of the Federal Maritime Commission need only consult with his colleagues on major appointments. A role in budgeting is also retained for commissions in most instances. In the Civil Aeronautics Board, Federal Power Commission, Federal Trade Commission, and Securities and Exchange Commission, authority is reserved to revise or approve budget estimates and to allocate appropriated funds among "major programs and purposes." In the Interstate Commerce Commission, budget authority is phrased somewhat differently but to the same effect. The members of the Federal Maritime Commission are given no role in budgeting.

Little is said regarding setting regulatory agendas and working priorities, forging substantive decisions of consequence, and handling external relationships. The clearest indication of a special role for the chairman in directing work at the staff level, important in all of these areas, is in the organizational orders of the Federal Maritime Commission. The chairman "administers the policies of the Commission to its responsible officials, and through conferences with and reports from such officials assures the efficient discharge of their responsibilities." Putting aside the Federal Communications Commission for a time again, in the remaining agencies there are at best vague indications of an undefined role for the chairman in directing staff work. Internal elaborations of the Civil Aeronautics Board, Federal Trade Commission, and Interstate Commerce Commission make some modest differentiations regarding roles in decision-making at the commission level. Chairmen, seemingly in the interest of the orderly conduct of business rather than for larger purposes, are assigned responsibility for commission meeting agendas and for presiding over those meetings. The chairman of the Interstate Commerce Commission may create and appoint commission committees. Also, the chairmen of the three agencies are to serve as the spokesmen for their colleagues, especially to Congress.

Of the six agencies discussed thus far, the chairmanship in the Federal Maritime Commission emerges as the most potent office. The charters enjoyed by chairmen in the other five agencies are quite similar in fundamental respects and are somewhat weaker. The formal position of chairman in the Federal Communications Commission is the weakest of the seven, although the statement of authority in the Communications Act is strong. The chairman is "the chief executive officer of the Commission." In addition to presiding at meetings of the commission and representing it in legislative matters and in relations with other governmental units, he is to "coordinate and organize the work of the Commission in such a manner as to promote prompt and efficient disposition of all matters within the jurisdiction of the Commission." Despite this language, the commission has limited the chairman severely through its own orders.

Administrative Order No. 11 relating to the commission was promulgated in 1956. Its origins are in periods when chairmen were felt by other members to be overbearing. The order remains as a very precise and detailed delineation of the relationship between the chairman and his colleagues. Three major categories of action are covered. The first consists of "internal matters of a fairly routine character." The chairman may take final action on these, although he is directed to inform the commission periodically as to what has been done. The illustrations incorporated into the order include: procurement; assignment of office space; position classification through GS-15; individual personnel actions through GS-9, except firings or actions pertaining to staff in commissioners' offices; administrative manuals; and "minor and non-substantive changes in operating procedure."

The second category pertains to matters which do not involve policy determinations, but which are of a non-routine character. The chairman may act, but he must specifically advise the commission of each action. Illustrations are: "work assignments to the staff of a substantial and unusual nature"; personnel ceilings; staffing schedules; initiation of or changes in administrative analysis or reporting systems; individual personnel actions in grades GS-10 through GS-14, with the same qualification noted previously; minor organizational changes within an existing bureau or office; and major changes in procedure.

The third category consists of matters of a policy character. In these, the role of the chairman is to prepare proposals for commission consideration. For matters originating in the staff, the chairman is to serve essentially as a conduit to the commission. Such proposals are to be addressed to the larger body through him, apparently to minimize his impact on them. Illustrations of policy matters include: budgetary requests; allotment of funds; "formal personnel policies"; "extraordinary assignments of personnel" (e.g., details outside the agency); major organizational changes within bureaus or offices, and all changes affecting two or more bureaus or offices; procedural changes of a "substantive" nature and those which concern the "protective" dimensions of the Communications Act and the Administrative Procedure Act; all involuntary personnel separations; and all actions affecting personnel at the GS-15 level or above or in the offices of commissioners.

Formal allocations of authority and responsibility must be extended into organization arrangements if they are to be utilized effectively. Organization for the performance of administrative and management functions is as much a part of basic charters as are statutory provisions and elaborations on them. Overall, however, the formal lines of authority and responsibility linking the commission and staff levels generally do not indicate much about operating relationships.[18] The Federal Communications Commission and the Federal Maritime Commission are exceptions. In the former, the chairman's role is defined in limited terms; in the latter, it is defined in expansive terms. In the other agencies, little is conveyed by organization charts and what may be imputed from them regarding the roles of chairmen and commissions in relation to key staff positions, especially those in line units. It is not certain, for example, whether the director of a particular bureau is responsible to the chairman or to the commission, or under what circumstances responsibility runs to one or the other.

Arrangements regarding administrative support functions are a partial exception. In each of the agencies, functions such as personnel, budgeting and fiscal management, records management, procurement, general administrative services, and, in most instances, data processing, are carried out in an organizational unit headed by an executive or managing director. Formal statements in five of the agencies indicate that these officials are responsible to the chairman. The managing director-secretary of the Civil Aeronautics Board "assists the chairman in discharging his functions as executive and administrative head of the agency." In the Federal Maritime Commission, Federal Trade Commission, Interstate Commerce Commission, and Securities and Exchange Commission, provisions specify that the directors of support units are subject to the authority of the chairman. The Federal Power Commission and the Federal Communications Commission present variations. The executive director of the Federal Power Commission is responsible to the commission in matters reserved to the commission and to the chairman in matters delegated to him. The executive director of the Federal Communications Commission is "directly responsible to the Commission," although he works under the "supervision" of the chairman, helping to carry out delegated executive and administrative functions. Thus, the relationships defined between chairmen and executive or managing directors emphasize the special role of the former in agency administration, except in the Federal Communications Commission.

The position of executive or managing director (hereafter referred to as executive director, except when reference specifically is to one with the title of managing director) is important in the relationship between chairmen and other top staff officials. The managing director of the Federal Maritime Commission administers the agency on a day-to-day basis in behalf of the chairman. In addition to exercising substantive decision-making responsibilities delegated to him by the agency, he directs the activities of line bureaus and offices. Although the offices of secretary, general counsel, and administrative law judges report to the chairman, they are subject to managerial direction and coordination from the office of the managing director. The executive directors of the Federal Power Commission and the Federal Trade Commission are designated as the "chief operating official[s]" of those agencies. In practice, they do not direct the work of the bureaus and offices in the manner of the managing director of the Federal Maritime Commission. Instead they generally oversee and coordinate the work of the various parts from a broad management perspective, paying particular attention to problems affecting resource utilization and productivity. Such designations of general responsibility have not been provided the managing director-secretary of the Civil Aeronautics Board, the managing director of the Interstate Commerce Commission, and the executive directors of the Federal Communications Commission and the Securities and Exchange Commission. Some elements of broad responsibility are present to be sure, but the charters are not as strong. These administrators are charged with coordinating staff activities, providing administrative leadership, and planning, reviewing, and presenting proposals for more effective performance. The weight that the term "chief operating official" carries is absent, but even so the assigned functions include much more than just administrative support narrowly defined. Broad management matters are a legitimate concern.[19]

Other types of staff units surround the commissioners and chairmen. In most instances, there are no formal indications of special responsibility to the chairman. Exceptions include the Civil Aeronautics Board, where the Office of Community and Congressional Relations, the Office of Plans, the Office of Information, and the Office of Consumer Advocate are overseen by the managing director–secretary. The secretary and the public information officer of the Federal Communications Commission operate under the general supervision of the executive director. The relevant arrangements in the Federal Maritime Commission have been mentioned. In the Federal Trade Commission, the executive director shares responsibility with the Office of Policy Planning and Evaluation for dealing with priority problems in case-handling.

There are several observations to be made regarding formal arrangements. Chairmen typically enjoy formal charters which recognize some need for focused responsibility in important areas of agency activity, especially concerning agency administration. The formal arrangements for organizing expertise and operating responsibilities in administrative and management areas and for linkages with the commission level tend to emphasize the role of chairmen rather than the role of commissions. Qualifications must be entered only for the Federal Communications Commission. The stringent restrictions imposed on the chairmanship in this agency are not characteristic; indeed, they are highly idiosyncratic.

Most of the commissions apparently have not been convinced of the importance or necessity of precisely defining the collective prerogatives of members in overall agency management. Also, they are reluctant to imply that in substantive matters the role of the chairman is any greater than that of his colleagues, although there is some limited recognition that in certain areas, such as external relationships, a special role for chairmen may be necessary. By silence on the point and lack of specification in the administrative realm, commissions leave considerable room for chairmen to act.

In summary, the charters and associated organizational arrangements are best seen as providing very general frameworks for agency governance, leaving much to be determined in the interactions involved in carrying out regulatory tasks and by the conventions and understandings that have developed over time. Much of the burden of the subsequent chapters is to examine how the formal charters are elaborated, and perhaps modified in application.

Into the Bog

Agency governance, as has been suggested previously, may be mapped through ascertaining patterns of involvement and relative influence of chairmen, commissioners, and top staff in critical choices and related processes. Analysis is burdened with considerable imprecision. Isolating critical choices—those that have significant implications for regulatory values and objectives—from other types is difficult. There is no claim that the task is executed with precision. The effort proceeds, however, informed by the distinctions and the importance of assessing patterns of involvement and influence in relation to the significance and nature of what is being decided.

Given the suggestion of extensive joint involvement of chairmen and members in making critical choices, the notions of influence and leadership are especially important to the analysis. A broad meaning is assigned to them, admittedly masking certain fine points regarding relationships among officials. Essentially, influence refers to the relationship among decision-makers which results in the behavior of one being determined or substantially affected in a purposive way by another. To exercise influence in an agency context is to affect decisions in substantial fashion.[20] Leadership refers to the exercise of extraordinary influence.[21] The extent to which chairmen are leaders is critical in the problem of agency governance. With the question of patterns in control, it bears directly on the degree to which conditions of "splintered management" and "multiple direction" remain characteristic.

The notions of influence and leadership applied in the analysis enfold phenomena which are at times set apart and discussed in terms of power and authority. Their connotations generally fit the situations under examination, especially as to the subtle nature of relationships among those who interact to produce decisions and the importance of persuasion as a means for shaping choices, in contrast to coercion, suggested by the term power, or command, suggested by the term authority.[22] But there are prerogatives associated with positions. From time to time, circumstances may justify references to authority, although in application, one of its most important uses is as a basis for influence, not command.

Influence does not just occur; its dynamics and its origins in organizational phenomena and in the characteristics of participants must be explored. A major point of curiosity is the relative importance of the two in agency governance. A tendency is apparent in government and elsewhere to explain variations in official behavior, and, in this instance, variations in influence within regulatory agencies, in terms of "personality," or to say that Jones has a greater impact than his associate Smith because he is more knowledgeable, aggressive, likeable, and energetic. Two major consequences flow from this proclivity. One is to mask the impact of organizational changes on patterns of influence within agencies. Another is to emphasize the "better man" approach to improving organizational performance. Both of these find important expression in the views of the Ash council.

Within the realm of organizational phenomena, patterns of influence among upper echelon officials in areas of critical choice may be understood in terms of three interrelated bases: the formal prerogatives of position; operative expectations regarding the behavior of various officials, that is, role; and the strategic resources associated with positions.[23] The formal prerogatives of position are set out in statutes, commission elaborations, and delegations and may affect the distribution of influence through providing a basis for independent action. Their more important effects may lie in their contributions, along with other factors, to conditioning the expectations found among chairmen, members, and staff as to their roles in agency processes. These expectations are especially important as they concern the degrees of influence and the quanta of leadership that are viewed as legitimate in those who fill the various positions.[24] In a sense, strategic resources are provided by formal prerogatives of position and notions of role. They concern access to and control over central aspects of agency decision-making activity, especially in regard to the information and the processes employed, including participation in decisions. They also concern the management of external relationships through information processing, representation, and negotiation. Strategic resources are important in two ways. First, they may be employed positively and directly to influence particular choices. Second, a sense of dependency in others resulting from perceived differentials in organizational location and in resources may, itself, serve as a resource in the exercise of influence through eliciting deference.[25]

The personal dimension of influence is more difficult to explore in a study such as this. It concerns things about persons that may be associated with susceptibility to being influenced as well as things about persons that are associated with the capacity to exercise influence. As to the latter, there are a number of characteristics that are often associated with a capacity to be influential. These include ambition, energy, intellectual ability, prestige brought to a position, and competence in role performance. Style and adeptness in interpersonal relations are often considered to be especially significant in the exercise of leadership in group as well as other settings.[26] Susceptibility to influence involves the perceptions of individuals regarding their organizational place and their related interests that become engaged in decision-making activities.

Influence or leadership occurs in relationships in which resources of participants, organizational and personal, are joined with individual interests or stakes in outcomes. In these relationships, certain interests may be served by attempting to exercise influence in the choices to be made, but interests may also be served by being influenced. Thus the relationships may be seen as involving, at least in part, exchanges in which something of value to an individual, a reward, or the avoidance of a sanction, may be gained by following the lead of another. The nature of the interests to be served are as complex as the notion of personality. Organizational interests may include the creation of an obligation to be reclaimed at a later time; service to a sense of institutional well-being; and maintaining communications channels. Interests more directly related to personality may also be involved, such as the avoidance of interpersonal conflict.

The chapters to follow will explore the nature and uses of the resources of principal agency participants in the regulatory process, with particular emphasis on chairmen and their colleagues. Chapters 3, 4, and 5 deal with areas of agency activity related to institutional character. More specifically, they treat control, influence, and leadership in decisions affecting organizational resources, structure, and processes. The next two chapters focus on decision-making in substantive regulatory matters through examining the direction of work at the staff level and decision-making at the commission level.

In all of these, much of the data employed come from interviews with sixty-eight present and former chairmen, commissioners, and staff and two additional close observers of the regulatory process conducted between September 1973 and January 1974. Their distribution by agency and position, or last position (if no longer with the agency), appears below. The interviews employed open-ended questions and lasted from thirty minutes to four hours, with most running approximately an hour and a quarter. Extensive notes

DISTRIBUTION OF INTERVIEWS

	CAB	FCC	FMC	FPC	FTC	ICC	SEC	Other
Chairman	4	3	1	1	4	2	2	
Member	1	1	—	2	3	1	1	
Staff	8	6	5	6	7	4	6	
Other								2
TOTAL	13	10	6	9	14	7	9	70

approaching a verbatim transcript were taken during each interview, then corrected and supplemented immediately thereafter. The nature of the interviewing strategy dictated by the circumstances was such that the potential for precise quantitative treatment of the data was limited. Their usefulness on the basic points of interest and for indicating the nuances of relationships is considerable, however. To a large extent, the interviewees were selected on the basis of their reputations as perceptive, knowledgeable, and candid observers of the regulatory process. Many, especially members and staff, had observed agency operations under a number of chairmen. Several of the chairmen interviewed had previously served as members, and some had served on both the staff and as members. In a world more generous, the interviews would have been greater in number and better distributed among agencies and types of officials. A very high degree of congruence in perceptions across the entire spectrum of interviews on major points of inquiry gives confidence in the reliability of that which is reported, however.

Liberal use is made of direct quotations from interviews in subsequent chapters. In most instances, they are attributed to persons by position rather than by name because of pledges of confidentiality. Whenever material appears in quotation marks without source specification, that material is from the interviews.

3.

Chairmen, Commissioners, and Agency Administration: An Overview

Speaking to a meeting of the Antitrust Law Section of the American Bar Association a few years ago, Miles W. Kirkpatrick, then chairman of the Federal Trade Commission, said:

> I should make it clear that in the management of the Commission's day-to-day affairs, there are no collegial decisions. Management of the Commission, save for the appointment of top policy making positions and policy decisions having to do with the allocation of major resources, is placed squarely on the Chairman. In my experience, matters having to do with the management of the Commission's staff are not the subject of debate among the Commissioners.[1]

But for others, regulatory agency management means continuing uncertainty regarding the allocation of administrative responsibilities and endless bickering about mundane matters, while the larger regulatory issues of the day are pushed aside. In order to determine which of these contrasting images captures reality, in this and the next two chapters, the relationship between chairmen and commissioners will be examined in decisions about ways and means for carrying out regulatory programs. The administrative functions of interest concern personnel and financial resources and organizational structure and processes.

Patterns

The general pattern in the relationship between chairmen and commissioners in decision-making concerning personnel and financial resources and organizational structure and processes is one in which chairmen tend to be preeminent while their colleagues' role is restricted. Table 1 summarizes the perceptions of those interviewed on three points: the engagement of members in administrative matters, an indication of their general interest and involvement; their general responsiveness to the leadership of chairmen in administrative matters; and the discretion enjoyed by chairmen in decision-making in these areas.[2]

TABLE 1

CHAIRMEN, COMMISSIONERS, AND ADMINISTRATIVE DECISIONS

	Engagement of Commissioners	*Responsiveness of Commissioners to the Chairman's Leadership*	*Discretion of the Chairman*
CAB	Moderate	High	Broad
FCC	Moderate	Moderate	Limited
FMC	Limited	High	Broad
FPC	Limited	High	Broad
FTC	Limited	High	Broad
ICC	Moderate	Moderate	Moderate
SEC	Limited	High	Broad

The characterizations generally hold true for the 1961–74 period, although there have been periodic aberrations, as in the case of the Federal Trade Commission in the late 1960s when Chairman Paul Rand Dixon was challenged seriously by his colleagues. They represent striking agreement among those interviewed with one exception. That exception is the Civil Aeronautics Board on the engagement of commissioners. In contrast to others associated with the agency, two former chairmen perceived the engagement of other members as more than limited, hence the moderate characterization.

The four agencies in which commissioners clearly are perceived to be engaged in administrative functions in a limited way, to be highly responsive to the leadership of chairmen, and in which chairmen have substantial discretion are the Federal Maritime Commission, the Federal Power Commission, the Federal Trade Commission, and the Securities and Exchange Commission. Interviews indicated that the most emphatic manifestation of preeminence is in the Federal Maritime Commission and is related to the potent base of formal authority provided that chairman. By all accounts the focus of Federal Maritime Commission members is almost exclusively on substantive proceedings. In the Federal Power Commission, according to one former chairman's assistant, "By and large, commissioners recognize administration to be in the chairman's domain." The result, as a former executive director put it, is that "other members are not involved in management." The Federal Trade Commission is the site of the only recent major, frontal challenge by members to the prerogatives of the chairman in management. This brief rebellion, which will be examined in some detail at later points, stands anachronistically outside the ordinary state of affairs existing in the agency. A top-level staff member, who has observed a number of chairmen at close range, reflected on his experience. "Under the reorganization plan, the chairman is responsible for the management of the commission. All members except one, since 1961, have fully recognized this responsibility. They did not want to get involved. They wish the chairman to be strong and assertive in administrative matters." Another former staff member with many years' experience saw "a general inclination to let the chairman have his way on administrative questions." And a former chairman reported, "I did not feel that other commissioners were involved in the management function, with rare exceptions."[3] Members of the Securities and Exchange Commission ordinarily have evidenced a hearty disdain and marked disinterest in nonsubstantive topics. Regarding administration, "On most matters, they are happy to have the chairman do it," according to a person who has served in that position. From the perspective of the commissioners themselves, in the words of one of that group, "Commissioners are not called upon and not involved unless it is a major question. Commissioners are not disturbed by the dominant role of the chairman."

The Civil Aeronautics Board might have been placed with these four agencies with justification. Two chairmen, a former board member who served through most of the period, and staff members whose experience in the agency spanned the entire period saw the engagement of members as consistently limited. According to a chairman, the others "are glad to have someone pick up that part of the load"; according to another, they are "delighted." Even the two chairmen who reported a moderate level of engagement saw colleagues as quite responsive. They did not feel their capacity to act to be unduly limited. In the words of one, "On a particular point a couple might disagree, but then say, 'But if you want it, O.K.'"

Moderate engagement on the part of Federal Communications

Commission and Interstate Commerce Commission members apparently has had constraining effects. It would be a mistake to interpret this
as meaning that the chairmanship in these agencies is impotent in administrative areas. For the Federal Communications Commission, the
characterizations in the table mask a certain ambivalence. Some elaboration on the point at the risk of anticipating subsequent sections
seems warranted. The formal restrictions surrounding the chairman
of the Federal Communications Commission have been discussed.
They represent an interest of commissioners in avoiding domination
by chairmen. But the domination that has been feared over the years
basically pertains to the substantive work of the agency. Although
individual commissioners may have real interests in nonsubstantive
matters, these are not the principal sources of the constraints. In a
way, the chairman's administrative capacity is held hostage in order
to protect the larger interests of the members, a conclusion substan-
tiated by little observable collective interest in agency management.
Ambivalence results from the recognition by members that chairmen
properly and necessarily have unique administrative responsibilities,
and a fear that they might carry them so far as to diminish the role of
members in areas that are important to them. A former commissioner
captured the ambivalence very well. "The commission resents it when
the chairman takes his administrative responsibilities too seriously.
But it expects him to assume ultimate responsibility for dull things
like the budget, space, and personnel." Within these perimeters, in
the "dull things," chairmen generally seem to prevail. He went on to
say, "Members may explain themselves, but chairmen generally are
not overruled." According to a former chairman, "The chairman
usually gets what he wants." Another who has viewed the Federal
Communications Commission from a number of perspectives in addition to that of the chair observed, "If the chairman consults, the
commission will go along." Thus, the interests of the commission
vis-à-vis the chairman do not preclude some discretion and a measure
of responsiveness to his leadership. The process of reaching the point
of colleague approval and action may be somewhat more onerous
than in the case of other agencies, however.

The Interstate Commerce Commission constitutes a departure of
a different sort. The chairman of that agency has not been as formally
constrained as has his Federal Communications Commission counterpart. Nor does the commission as a whole manifest even a moderate
level of true engagement in administrative matters. Most members of
the Interstate Commerce Commission are engaged only in the most
limited sense, are highly responsive to the leadership of the chairman,
and are willing to allow the chairman a large slice of discretion. Certain proprietary interests and substantial engagement of some senior

members lead to the table's characterization. Their experience is rich and deep in Interstate Commerce Commission matters and includes years under the previous rotational arrangement and service as chairman in that scheme. Their present interests are tied to positions at the division level of the commission. Commissioner Virginia Mae Brown indicated some of the implications of traditional sensitivities for Interstate Commerce Commission chairmen, and particularly for the then chairman George Stafford, when asked if the chairman could become more powerful.

> All of us would begin to sit here and watch. We'd all be ready to jump on him. Perhaps he wouldn't have done anything wrong, yet, but we'd be watching. And every time he did something we didn't like, we'd call him down to conference and change the rules and regulations so he couldn't do it again. That's happened to chairmen who have just sat for a year. Now we've never done it to George, and they didn't do it to me but I've been here when they've done it to chairmen.[4]

Notwithstanding the interests of others and a need for caution, the chairman enjoys significant freedom of action. Even before 1969, the "commission expected the chairman to handle administrative matters on a day-to-day basis," according to one who served as chairman during that time.[5] Members coming to the commission in recent years are seen as fairly generous regarding the prerogatives of the chair. As a result, according to a member, "Most commissioners are reluctant to overrule the chairman in administrative matters." "Regarding administration and management, the chairman has pretty much a free hand," a close observer concluded.

The characterizations generally indicate that in the several agencies, more often than not the swath of chairmen in administrative matters is as wide, if not wider, than that anticipated by the formal charters. Chairmen appear to be preeminent. The exceptions are the Federal Communications Commission and, to a lesser extent, the Interstate Commerce Commission. Even in these, the office is potent. Formal prerogatives of position are important sources of preeminence, but other sources also may be discerned.

Roots of Preeminence

The important place of chairmen in administration is rooted in statutory assignments of authority, in expectations held within the agencies as to what chairmen should do, in the strategic resources associated with the chairmanship, and in the nature of commissioners' interests. Chairmen in the five agencies are preeminent in decisions about organizational resources, structure, and processes because the

participant's generally shared expectations regarding the deportment
of chairmen are marked by a broad view concerning the legitimate
reach of the position; because the resources which chairmen have at
their disposal for influencing decisions are much more potent than
those which can be mobilized by other members, individually or collectively; and because the interests of other members, on the whole,
are best served by restraint. In the Federal Communications Commission and the Interstate Commerce Commission, the mix is such that
chairmen are somewhat circumscribed. Their capacity remains impressive, however, and the disparity between their influence and that
of their colleagues is substantial.

Expectations

There may not be perfect agreement about boundaries delineat-
ing the places of chairmen and commissioners in agency administration. But the expectation that the domain and possibilities of chairmen will be much richer and greater is generally shared by chairmen,
members, and staff. Operating arrangements in which the role of
chairman is primary and that of the commission as a whole is secondary are considered to be entirely appropriate, or legitimate. The
accepted differential may not be as great in larger issues such as
major agency reorganizations, but it is substantial. Ultimate responsibility of the collegium is not rejected, but it assumes a sense that is
vague. Despite this, it may collide from time to time with the expectations of primacy in the chair and produce tension. Conflict possibilities are limited, however, because administrative matters are rarely
viewed by members as significant enough to override the tendency to
exercise ultimate responsibility through the instrument of the collegium, the chairman.

Three foundations of the expectations that produce an expansive
role for chairmen are apparent: law, necessity, and organizational
routines. Laws promulgated by institutions seen as acting within their
legitimate sphere are at the least highly persuasive behavioral cues. A
belief in the legitimacy of statutory arrangements itself may result in
compliance, even if the substance of the arrangement is thought to
be unwise. To behave otherwise would be to violate the rules of the
game. Congress has distinguished the role of chairmen from that of
other members.[6] Commissioners generally believe that they should
play by the rules, even when the results are not to their liking, an
orientation expressed very clearly by one who served for several
years. In his view, too much power was vested in the chairman of his
agency as a result of a 1950 reorganization. Even prior to his nomina-
tion to the commission, he felt that a larger role for the commission

in the management of agency affairs was preferable. When offered an appointment, he considered whether in light of his views he could accept. The commissioner concluded that if he did accept, he assumed an obligation to live by the arrangements that existed and to recognize the primacy of the chairman. Ultimately, of course, he did accept, and he did play by the rules, even though he felt them to be misguided.

Reinforcement is provided by the presidential designation of chairmen. All the members enjoy presidential appointment, but the chairman has been named to exercise leadership responsibilities. He has been set apart from his colleagues by the president and has been given special status. That status distinction adds to the position a symbolic dimension with potent evocative capacity. It accentuates the specifications of formal authority and perhaps combines with them in symbiotic fashion.

Necessity as a foundation for an extensive role for chairmen in administrative matters concerns the notion that efficiency and effectiveness in regulatory administration require centralized responsibility for and authority over certain agency operations. Membership on a collegial body does not erase the rather general belief in the relationship between diffusion of responsibility and authority and inept administration. A former commissioner's assertion that "you need a strong chairman for administrative purposes" suggests the logic involved.

In addition to a predisposition to play by the larger rules of the game and a perceived association between centralized responsibility and integrated authority and efficiency and effectiveness, there are expectations stimulated by encounters with organizational routines. In contrast to the former commissioner who had rather firm opinions about the 1950 reorganization plans, most recent appointees have not given serious prior thought to the issue of authority for agency management. The battles of past years regarding the role of chairmen are at most historical fragments in the mind, not living controversies. Upon taking office, new members do not encounter a few sentences in relatively general statutory language regarding the chairmanship. They begin immediately to experience organizational routines that have developed based on those provisions, routines that emphasize the centrality of the chairmanship and that are woven into institutional fabrics. At the commission level, for example, the new member sees the chairman presiding, initiating, and representing the agency to the world outside. And he has little choice but to accept an important role for the chairman and the basic divisions of authority and responsibility that are in place.[7] If experience alters initial views, the time of departure is probably near.[8]

It would be a grand oversimplification to assert that all members of the independent regulatory agencies accept the preeminence of chairmen in key administrative areas to the same extent and for the same reasons. No doubt there are important variations in what commissioners expect. The interviews do suggest, however, a central tendency to accept a very large role for the chairman in decisions about organizational resources, structure, and processes.

Strategic Resources

The strategic resources which appear to be important in administrative decision-making fall into two general categories: knowledge resources and process resources. Knowledge resources consist of information about agency operations and particular matters to be decided and of expertise in budgeting, personnel, organization, and other administrative areas. Process resources are those which may be employed to influence how decisions are made. Externally imposed requirements dictate many decisions, and established organizational routines often govern such elements as timing and participation. But extensive room remains for shaping decision-making processes and, consequently, for influencing the decisions that result. Some of the process choices which may have substantive significance include initiation, or identification of a matter as requiring attention; definition of a problem and the alternatives for dealing with it; and specification of the organizational route to be followed to decision, participation along the way, responsibility for the final choice, and how the choice will be implemented.

The knowledge and process resources associated with the position of chairman are rather large, and those associated with the position of commissioner are rather limited under ordinary circumstances. Chairmen have extensive access to knowledge stores, both outside the agency and within it, whereas the access of other members is limited. Commissioners have at best a modest capacity to influence the decisional flow, whereas chairmen have rather rich opportunities. Fundamental to both conditions is the staff support which the chairman commands. Executive directors and the heads of bureaus and offices report to chairmen on administrative matters on a regular, continuing basis. In contrast, the flow of information from staff to other members is irregular, limited in scope, and often after the fact. The relevant technical skills, located in staff units, are tied to the chairman's office and linked only loosely to the offices of other commissioners.

Staff assistants to both the chairman and the members are important connections between the top level and staff operations. The difference in the number of staff assistants to chairmen and to members is ordinarily not large, although there have been instances of significant disparities. But a small difference may be important if it results in freeing even a single staff member from immersion in cases for attention to other matters. Usually there is a special or executive assistant on the staff of the chairman who has major responsibilities of this type. Persons in these positions often act as deputy chairmen. They maintain close touch with operations at the staff level, and they are especially, though not exclusively, concerned with administrative problems. They facilitate the flow of information to the chairman and the mobilization of expertise in attacking problems. In contrast, the major responsibilities of the assistants to members are in the case decision area. They may develop information about administrative affairs through informal contacts with other staff, but the flow of information to members that results bears the same characteristics as that from the formal reporting system: irregularity and incompleteness. The capacity of the offices of members to tap technical skills relevant to administrative questions is limited as well.[9]

Staff tied to the office of the chairman are also important conduits for information from outside sources, as are chairmen themselves. Information originating in other parts of government—in Congress, the Office of Management and Budget, the Civil Service Commission, and in other agencies with which there are working relationships—comes to them rather than to commissions.

Commissioners realize that the knowledge resources available to chairmen are superior in scope, depth, quality, and timeliness of reception. The sense that the chairman knows more adds to predispositions to approve his recommendations and to accept his actions.

The members of a commission have almost no capacity to affect processes pertaining to administrative functions until matters are brought to them. Important preliminary determinations often take place beyond their reach, even those concerning whether a decision is to be made by them or by someone else. In the gray areas, chairmen decide whether to involve their colleagues or not. Overall, the interviews indicate that chairmen have wide latitude in process choices, including those affecting the nature and extent of commission participation. As one put it, other members appear quite willing "to support the chairman's exercise of discretion as to what to take to the commission." A former member who served for a number of years reported that at the start, when he and several other members and the chairman were new, there were, for a time, "fights" about what should be on the agenda. "Ultimately, we decided that the chairman had to do it. Reliance has to be placed on his fairness." In this situation, as it turned out, matters of moment, such as significant organizational changes, would be raised and resolved without the knowledge of the members. They learned about them from comments by the staff at commission meetings, after the fact.

Even when administrative matters are taken to commissions, chairmen control the timing. Questions may be presented for consideration when most advantageous for securing acceptance of the chairman's position. The resource can and sometimes is used in a manipulative way. Presentation close to action-forcing deadlines, as in the case of budgets, is not unknown. Few options beyond approval are open to commissions when faced with the need for immediate action and limited information.

Probably the most significant means readily available for members to employ collectively are to delay or to refuse to act once a matter is before them. The instances in which commissioners have influenced administrative decisions indicate, however, that the effective resources are not likely to be collective in character, but those of an individual member, such as special knowledge in budgeting.

Interests

The expectations of commissioners in the administrative realm suggest some constraints on the development of collective resources and on vigor in the employment of individual resources in ways that would challenge the preeminence of chairmen. An examination of the relevant interests of commissioners will suggest additional reasons for their limited impact on agency administration.

Pertinent interests can be classified as those served by avoidance of administrative matters and those which are served by involvement. Interests served by avoidance are freedom from tedium, time for "important" things, career development, good relations with colleagues and staff, and the capacity to influence decisions deemed to be significant.

Perhaps the most consistent characterization of commissioners of all the agencies is that they are bored by agency administration..In the Interstate Commerce Commission, there is "no interest," according to a commissioner. In the Federal Communications Commission, as a close observer characterized the situation, "the executive director is lucky to get two hours for a budget presentation and four members to attend." Even though the commission has reserved extensive responsibilities to itself, Nicholas Johnson, who served as a commissioner, charged that these are met with a periodic "collective nod," not with sustained attention.[10] A reluctance to take time away from substantive pursuits that are more intriguing and which seem more significant and rewarding is generally apparent. The time required for the preliminary and preparatory work that enlarges a capacity to influence decisions in a systematic and substantial way is not expended.

Long-term career interests may reinforce tendencies toward avoidance. For members who see themselves as serving for a limited period, then moving on, the investment of time and energy in administrative problems may not make much sense. If one is "passing through" and wishes to make the most of the opportunity, whether in terms of substantive impact or public visibility, lavishing attention on such matters may, indeed, be counter-productive.

Interests are served by restraint, even for those who see themselves as career commissioners. If one or a group attempt to alter patterns of limited involvement, a high level of tension and conflict would almost certainly be produced among colleagues and staff. Challenges to the chairmanship would unquestionably have such effects and, in addition, would most likely fail. A harmonious working environment is valued by most commissioners. The small and intimate settings in which they work magnify the importance of interpersonal relationships. As one who did suffer the pains associated with a challenge to a chairman described his own feelings, there is a natural inclination to want to be a "team man." Even on substantive issues of unquestionable importance, affiliative interests tend to restrain position-taking and strategies which would raise conflict to a high level. A strong challenge to a chairman on an administrative point, and particularly as to the nature and scope of his prerogatives, runs the almost sure risk of alienating colleagues and the key staff members who identify with him, plus those who place a high priority on harmony. The mood that results was characterized by an observer of the nonreaction of Federal Maritime Commission members to the initiation of significant organizational changes by a chairman without informing them beforehand. When asked to explain their silence, he responded, "Why create bad feelings? Why argue for the sake of argument?"

Challenges may result in more than bad feelings. They may result in the loss of tangible benefits that chairmen can distribute. These include travel, including foreign travel; facilitating the operation of the member's own office; making adjustments in the agenda to fit the convenience of a member; and providing a general sense of inclusion in the work of the commission through disseminating information and opportunities for participation beyond formal case work. The good will of chairmen is important in other respects. Their views may be perceived as having weight in reappointment decisions. The chairman's support for positions on substantive matters of importance to a commissioner or commissioners can be critical. A loss of access to the chairman and his influence is in itself a serious diminution of the influence of the individual member over the course of regulatory affairs.

Clearly, then, a variety of interests discourage the involvement of commissioners in agency administration, particularly when involvement might mean challenging the chairman. These interests, operating in the first instance on individual commissioners, by extension discourage groups of commissioners from collectively building, mobilizing, and employing resources in the administrative area.

Other interests have an opposite effect and must be added to the scale. They are informational, institutional, decisional, instrumental, and allocational in character. Informational interests are in knowing about agency conditions from an administrative perspective and about important decisions in this area. They are rooted in the natural concern of members who have considerable responsibility for agency well-being. There are two related aspects of informational interests. The first is curiosity about organizational conditions, problems, and prospective alterations. The second and perhaps stronger is the avoidance of surprise about especially important decisions, ignorance of which might be translated into embarrassment, given collective responsibility.

Institutional interests concern the well-being of the agency as a whole. They may be present in particular administrative decisions such as the selection of top staff members, but as a motivation for members they are most important when agencies are under attack for management deficiencies. For example, during the early 1960s when there was extensive criticism of the rather majestic backlogs of some of the commissions, the members of several collectively became quite deeply involved in the problem and possible remedies.

Decisional interests relate to that which most commissioners see as their principal function: making choices in the formal substantive matters that are brought for consideration. The major interest here, according to a member, is that "commissioners are presented material for decision-making." Conditions which impede the flow of material, then, may become matters of collective concern.

Instrumental interests do not concern administrative matters per se, but the use of administrative decisions to influence other determinations. An example would be taking an initial negative position on a top-level appointment in order to establish a bargaining point in a substantive matter being considered concurrently.

Allocational interests are in the distribution of agency resources among various program elements and the well-being of elements for which a member has special affection. There has been continuing conflict among Federal Trade Commission members for several years concerning the allocation of resources to enforce the Robinson-Patman Act, an example of interests of this type at work. The salience of allocational interests is enhanced when commission members have special responsibilities for segments of an agency's activities, as in the Interstate Commerce Commission and Federal Communications Commission.[11]

When the interests of commissioners which are served by involvement in administrative matters and those which are served by restraint or avoidance are weighed, it is apparent that a basis for comprehensive, continuous, and in-depth involvement of individual members and of commissions is weak. Some interests associated with involvement may be shared by members generally and thus may constitute a basis for collective action. But the dominant characteristic is their individualistic quality. They may be satisfied most effectively by members acting alone rather than together, further limiting possibilities for joint efforts.

The most pronounced sense of collective member interest in the administrative sphere is found in the Federal Communications Commission, followed by the Interstate Commerce Commission. The interests of Federal Communications Commission members do not concern agency administration as such, but interests which are affected by agency administration in a tangential way. The size of the commission, seven members, in conjunction with its highly charged political environment, creates an extraordinary need for internal and external visibility, according to one interpretation. There is a strong collective interest in the maintenance of organizational conditions which enhance visibility. One means is the retention of extensive collective prerogatives in administration and their periodic assertion.

In the Interstate Commerce Commission, size and volume of work long ago dictated extensive delegation of authority to subsidiary units. The three divisions of the commission have been significant decision-making bodies for many years. A pattern of decentralized attention to administrative matters developed, fitting the divisional arrangement for decision-making. Both, it can be argued, reflect collective interests in facilitating the handling of the commission's considerable case load. Even prior to 1969 and presidential appointment of the chairman, administrative responsibilities were becoming more centralized. But a residual sense of collective interests in decentralized processes and consequently some limitations on the chairman have continued through the years, though considerably diminished in strength. A keen student of the contemporary situation concluded that, "On balance, their (the members') interests are not significant, important, or constraining."

The foregoing discussion has suggested that the limited or mod-

erate engagement of agency members in administrative matters can
be understood in large part in terms of generous expectations regarding the chairmanship, the disparity in the relative strategic resources
of chairmen and members, and the limited interests of members.
When there is involvement, it is generally cursory and *pro forma,*
most often resulting in approval through formal commission action
or informal clearance of matters previously decided by chairmen and
their aides. More serious and vigorous involvement may be stimulated
from time to time, but it tends to be episodic, aimed at limited objectives, and more often than not represents individual rather than collective interests of members. This is the case even in the Federal
Communications Commission and the Interstate Commerce Commission, where the strongest sense of collective interests with operational
implications are to be found.

Consultation and Administrative Decision-making

The involvement of commissioners in administrative decision-
making is through consultation to a large extent. There are several
types of consultative relationships between chairmen and members.
One type is the consultation which precedes formal commission
decisions—ordinarily based upon recommendations coming from the
staff and the chairman. Matters precipitating consultation of this type
may be regularly and predictably before the commission, as in the
case of budgets and some appointments, or they may fall outside the
established routine, as in the case of a major reorganization proposal.
They may also vary in terms of importance, ranging from the most
mundane to the highly significant. Another type of consultation involves discussion in a formal setting, but without formal decision by
the commission. Discussions serve to elicit the opinions and reactions
of commissioners to problems and potential actions and have information exchange, reaction-testing and advice-giving as their major
functions. Consultation with members may also occur on an individual basis for similar purposes. This type may serve the added function
of securing the support of particular commissioners for a recommendation to come before the full body. A final type of consultation
simply involves one-way transmission of information from the chairman and staff to other members. Settings range from the formal
sessions of the commission to the most casual of encounters.

The scope and depth of the involvement of commissioners in
decision-making through consultative processes is difficult to specify
exactly. Nevertheless, some things can be said. Figure 1 is a graphic
suggestion of the relative magnitude of consultative and nonconsulta-
tive determinations in administrative matters. Most decision-making

in this area falls beyond the reach of commissions and in the domain of chairmen and staff. In addition to matters that are mandated to the attention of commissions, usually there will be consultation on only the most important questions regarding organizational resources, structure, and processes.

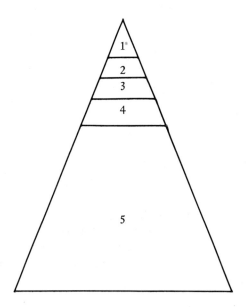

1. Formal decision by commission.

2. Discussion by full commission.

3. Discussion on individual basis.

4. One-way transmission of information to commissioners.

5. Noninvolvement.

Fig. 1. Estimated Proportion of Administrative Decision-making Involving Consultative Processes

Most consultation essentially involves the one-way transmission of information and perhaps does not truly deserve the term. Nevertheless, keeping the membership informed about major developments seems to be the most frequent meaning assigned by regulators. Information transmission tends to come at a late stage, after the initial attention of the chairman and staff. Options have been sifted and a course of action has been selected by the time the commission has become involved. Whatever form it may assume, consultation generally does not involve commissioners in the fundamentals of problems and alternatives or the significant exercise of choice. Its major (but not exclusive) function is securing the approval and legitimation of the choices of chairmen and staff.

There are differences in the nature and reach of consultative processes, however. Table 2 characterizes the consultative orientations

TABLE 2

CONSULTATIVE ORIENTATIONS OF CHAIRMEN: 1961–74

	Highly Consultative	Consultative	Minimally Consultative
CAB	2	2	1
FCC	2	3	–
FMC	–	2	1
FPC	–	1	2
FTC	1	3	1
ICC	1	–	–
SEC*	1	3	–

*Bradford Cook is not included because of his brief tenure.

of chairmen serving in the seven agencies during the 1961–74 period, based upon perceptions reported in the interviews. The orientations are indicated as highly consultative, consultative, or minimally consultative. Several interpretative comments are suggested by the table. There is considerable variation in the extent of consultation on administrative matters in the federal regulatory establishment, and there are significant variations in the recent experience of each agency. A complex of factors are involved. Institutional characteristics may be related to differences among agencies. No Federal Communications Commission chairman was placed in the minimally consultative category. Restrictions on the chairmanship force a significant amount of interaction with colleagues. None of the three persons who chaired the Federal Maritime Commission is characterized as highly consultative. The extensive formal authority placed in the chairmanship may preclude the necessity to consult extensively.

The most important point which may be drawn from the variations is the suggestion that the personal orientations of chairmen are a major determinant of the extent of consultation. They interact with other factors to produce the relationships and practices which exist at a particular time. The intensity of member interest in being consulted is one. The internal conditions resulting from the approach of a predecessor comprise another. The tensions that were evident at the end of Joseph S. Swidler's tenure as chairman of the Federal Power Commission and Paul Rand Dixon's as chairman of the Federal Trade Commission may have served to emphasize the consultative inclinations of Lee White and Caspar W. Weinberger who followed them. Yet another is serious attack on the agency from the outside, which may enlarge the scope and depth of consultation in order to mobilize fully the resources of the agency for defensive purposes.

There is a corollary point to the suggestion of the importance of the personal orientations of chairmen in determining the amount and nature of consultation. Extensive capacities reside in the chairmanship to control consultative processes. Decisions of chairmen about when and when not to consult are to a great extent discretionary. A comment from a study of the role of federal regulatory officials in the 1960s reported the following statement by a member of the Federal Trade Commission:

> The FTC chairman does not call in and consult the other commissioners concerning important matters . . . . The commission as an entity does not have the power to direct personnel or the flow of work. These things depend on the chairman. One problem is to determine what is major policy. In the case of the FTC, however, the chairman has labeled things as administrative matters which should be called major policy matters.[12]

The chairman during this period was Paul Rand Dixon. In contrast, the approach of Miles W. Kirkpatrick, whose chairmanship closely followed that of Dixon's and who served with the same commissioners as Dixon for the most part, was quite different. Kirkpatrick commented that, in his view, "When matters are *arguably* policy, there is not just consultation, but they are brought up for formal consideration." No doubt Kirkpatrick was influenced by the considerable tension that had developed between several members and Dixon. Just as certainly the contrast reflects different notions of the appropriate relationship a chairman should maintain with his colleagues.

Interesting differences in consultation may be noted even when decisions clearly are the chairman's to make. On such matters, for example, Kirkpatrick "almost never consulted prior to action." His successor, Lewis Engman, consulted on an individual basis, guided by his perceptions of the interests of commissioners and their potential contribution to the resolution of the question under consideration. Another set of contrasts may be drawn from the Securities and Exchange Commission. Even on major appointments, former chairman Manuel Cohen is said to have "told the commissioners what he was going to do." Ray Garrett, Jr., a successor who served as chairman from 1973 to 1975, "would consult on appointments even if the reorganization plan did not require it." He did consult on appointments he could have made alone.

What difference does it make whether a chairman consults extensively or minimally? The act of consultation, no matter in what form, generally does not require chairmen or their agents to alter an established position or to revise a proposed course of action. Extensive consultation cannot be said to limit the discretion of chairmen in significant fashion. A low level of consultation allows chairmen to proceed without the necessity to explain or justify decisions. The consequences are a marginal enlargement of discretion and, possibly, a long-term, adverse impact on morale and the climate of the relationship with colleagues.

Paradoxically, consultation, rather than limiting the influence of chairmen, may constitute a resource for the exertion of influence, even beyond administrative matters. The paradox takes form from perhaps the most important operating sense of consultation—the flow of information from the chairman to other commissioners, not joint decision-making. Consultation means keeping the other commissioners informed and "touching bases." Members recognize the substantial role of the chairman in administrative matters and that he may hold the relevant cards very closely to his vest if he wishes. For a chairman to consult is to extend a "courtesy" to members and to recognize their unique position in the agency and their ultimate responsibility. The courtesy of consultation extended by chairmen often is felt to require a courteous response. It generates an obligation to agree or support what is proposed in exchange for recognition of the special place of colleagues. A close observer of the Interstate Commerce Commission noted, on the basis of reasoning very close to this, "It is not difficult for a chairman to have his way on management matters if he consults." A study of the Federal Trade Commission concluded:

> The key factor is consultation. Where the chairman asserts his full authority aggressively, commissioners tend to feel demoted and unable to play their proper role. Where a chairman carefully consults his fellow commissioners concerning major decisions and uses his powers cautiously, the members are glad to be rid of the administrative routine.[13]

The possibility of consultation as resource rather than a constraint is one reason why many chairmen do not see the concept of ultimate collegial responsibility as an impediment to their ambitions or as a hindrance to their leadership in administrative decision-making.

There are other positive values that chairmen often associate with consultation. They do not always feel certain that they and the staff have complete and sure command of each situation in which a decision must be made. The contributions of colleagues and a joint decision may be considered advantageous. Consultation not infrequently results in constructive suggestions coming from men of experience and judgment. Finally, consultation in administrative matters contributes to the development and maintenance of a temper and tone at the summit of the agency that facilitates decision-making in the substantive realm.

4.

Organizational Resourses

A major objective in strengthening regulatory agency chairmanships during past years was to focus authority and responsibility for decisions about organizational resources. An examination of the relationship between chairmen and their colleagues in this context is a test of the effects of the changes. Another utility is involved. Personnel and budgeting are the administrative matters in which commissioners tend to be involved most consistently and in which they have the greatest interest. Examination of relationships in decisions concerning them should be particularly instructive in regard to the relative place of chairman and members in agency governance.

Personnel Resources

Decisions regarding personnel resources may be divided between those concerning general personnel policy and those concerning specific personnel actions, such as appointment, transfer, and promotion. Commissioners share responsibility for formulating agency personnel policy within the context of government-wide laws and regulations. In practice, little collective attention is given to broad considerations of, for example, recruitment practices or manpower utilization. From time to time, specific issues with general policy implications may arise, as in one agency recently when a prospective appointment precipitated consideration of the extent to which retired military officers should be employed. For the most part, personnel policy matters are not to be found in the formal or informal agendas of the commissions. Policies that guide discretionary action ordinarily are forged by chairmen and staff.

The most important personnel function of the commissions is to appoint or approve the appointment of persons in certain positions. Their engagement in personnel matters is almost exclusively to be found here. Consequently, attention will be given principally to the relationship between chairmen and commissioners in the appointment process.

Those positions for which commissions reserve a role in appointment are not always defined clearly. The statutes provide that "heads of major administrative units" are subject to approval in the Civil Aeronautics Board, Federal Communications Commission, Federal Power Commission, Federal Trade Commission, Interstate Commerce Commission, and Securities and Exchange Commission. No such statement is included in the Federal Communications Act. The chairman of the Federal Maritime Commission is required only to "consult" with colleagues on major appointments. The identification of "major administrative units" is left to the commissions in each case. Specification is to be found in formal decisions, policy statements, and customs. Both the Federal Maritime Commission and the Securities and Exchange Commission rely entirely on custom. The matter is not so critical in the Federal Maritime Commission, where the obligation of the chairman, generally met, is only to consult, based upon his notion of when commission consideration is warranted. A statement drawn from a 1969 inquiry into the chairman's appointment power described the approach of the Securities and Exchange Commission in the following manner:

> By longstanding practice the Commission as a whole appoints all division directors, all super-grades except Hearing Examiners and all associate division directors, plus the heads of all "offices" and their associate directors. In addition, the directors of all regional offices are appointed by the Commission as a whole, but there is a hazy area regarding the deputy regional directors. Apparently it is not required, but the previous Chairman did clear such appointments with his colleagues.[1]

Elaborations found in formal actions of the Federal Communications Commission, Federal Power Commission, and Interstate Commerce Commission were discussed previously. To recapitulate briefly, the Federal Communications Commission arrangements found in Administrative Order Number 11 are quite precise and restrictive in regard to the authority of the chairman. The Interstate Commerce Commission provisions are fairly precise, but less restrictive. The Federal Power Commission's administrative manual provides that appointments as "the heads of bureaus, offices and divisions and all hearing examiners" require commission approval.[2] But the 1969 inquiry indicated that other appointments were approved also.

Specifically reserved for appointment by the Commissioners as a whole are

all positions of Hearing Examiner, all super-grade positions, and all heads of
administrative units such as bureaus, divisions, and offices, and the deputies
to all of these officials. This includes the regional engineers and their deputies,
who head the various regional offices.[3]

As a result, Federal Power Commission members have a larger role in
appointments than their counterparts in most other agencies.

The organizational manual of the Civil Aeronautics Board repeats
statutory language regarding board approval. However, the 1969 study
indicates that the board has gone further in definition. It states:

Many years ago the Board adopted an internal rule that division chiefs and
up are subject to appointment by the entire board. All below this rank would
be appointed by the Chairman alone. The definition of "division chief" includes the heads of "offices," such as budget, personnel, management
analysis, . . .[4]

The Federal Trade Commission is the final agency to be considered. During the 1960s, Chairman Paul Rand Dixon's position was
that the "heads of major administrative units" included only the secretary, executive director, general counsel, and the directors of bureaus
and that the commission had no role in other appointments. Near the
end of Dixon's time as chairman, a majority of the commissioners
voted to extend the category to include sixty-three positions, arguing
that the definitional prerogative was theirs and that sixty-three was
the number of critical positions requiring approval.[5] The issue was
not resolved until Caspar W. Weinberger became chairman in 1969,
and then with some assistance from the U.S. Civil Service Commission. Principally relying on concepts of grade-level and on position
descriptions, it was suggested that persons in grades GS-16, GS-17,
and GS-18 who headed major organizations not within a bureau, or
who headed a bureau, should be considered to be head of a "major
administrative unit" and subject to commission approval. This
calculus brought two additional positions, program review officer
and director, Office of Hearing Examiners, into the commission's
approval orbit, a much more modest extension than that proposed.[6]

Thus some commissions have been more careful than others in
defining the appointments subject to approval. And given the fact
that practice does not always conform to formal specifications, it
may be concluded that the matter generally is not one of great concern. Furthermore, appointment to some positions is subject to
approval in some instances and not in others. The appointments of
administrative law judges are subject to approval in the Federal Communications Commission, the Federal Power Commission, and the
Interstate Commerce Commission, but not in the other agencies.
Deputies or assistants to the heads of major units are subject to

approval in the Federal Communications Commission and the Federal Power Commission.

Except in the Federal Communications Commission, where a variety of personnel actions must come before the commission, personnel decisions other than top-level appointments are made by chairmen and staff without commission involvement. The individual interests of commissioners may be tapped from time to time, resulting in participation of a sort, most often concerning their own offices. Personal associations may also stimulate involvement, as in support for a particular staff member for advancement. Expressions of support generally are based upon past association such as service in the members' office. At times, though infrequently, commissioners may serve as channels for outside applicants, perhaps at the request of a member of Congress.

Initiatives by members are rare in filling positions and, according to those who make such decisions, have declined considerably in number over the years. When there are expressions of interest, the behavior of members can best be characterized as restrained. There is general acceptance of established procedures and that such matters fall in the domain of chairmen and staffs. As might be suspected from the authority which the Federal Communications Commission has reserved, the pattern of declining interest and restraint has been less marked there, even in connection with lower-level appointments. The interests asserted, however, are quite limited in relation to the total range of personnel activities.

Generally, in personnel determinations that do not involve top-level appointments, members become engaged infrequently and more in the role of petitioners than as decision-makers. Chairmen personally and through the staff are unquestionably much more influential. Under ordinary circumstances, however, chairmen leave personnel matters beyond top-level appointments to the staff. Chairmen who do give direction to personnel activity may have a great impact on their agencies. The Federal Trade Commission provides an instructive example of the effects that may be caused, in this instance through policies guiding the recruitment of staff attorneys and the retention of personnel. Critical assessments of the commission during the 1960s pointed to a strategy for recruitment of attorneys attributed to Chairman Paul Rand Dixon as a major source of agency difficulties. Exclusion of the top graduates of prestigious, generally eastern law schools, it was alleged, adversely affected staff quality and regulatory efforts. Furthermore, personnel policies linked to the chairman protected long-time employees who were not fulfilling their responsibilities.[7] Dixon's successor, Caspar Weinberger, was no less interested in personnel matters and these occupied a considerable portion of his time.

He approached the commission as the regulatory counterpart of the
Augean stables and set forces in motion that ultimately caused the
replacement of more than half of the 1,500 employees. He also
instituted a recruitment policy that emphasized employment of the
most qualified attorneys. Significant changes came to be made in
staff composition, and in large part through them, in the manner in
which the commission performed.[8]

The recruitment and appointment of high-level staff members is
especially important from the standpoint of agency governance. Their
views shape critical regulatory choices in important and direct ways.
The circumstances of their selection affect subsequent relations with
chairmen and members. Those interviewed agreed that the gap between the influence of chairmen and commissioners in these appointments is quite wide, so wide as to place chairmen clearly in a leadership position. The common condition is for chairmen to make appointments and for their colleagues to ratify them.

Commissioners ordinarily become involved at the end of the
selection process. Initial determinations concerning the regulatory
orientations and other attributes to be sought in appointees are
made by the chairman and his staff. Those to be considered seriously
are identified with only limited participation by commissioners, even
when their suggestions are welcome. Commission participation begins
when a small number of finalists have been selected, or more typically,
after the chairman has decided upon his first choice. Then that
choice is presented for interviews with the other members as a
courtesy prior to submittal of a name for approval.

Almost no instances were pointed to during the 1961–74 period
in which chairmen were unable to secure commission acceptance of
their selections. In most cases, approval comes automatically after
routine consideration. The characteristic tone of the process was suggested by a former Federal Power Commission member's description
of the treatment of appointments during his nine years there. "The
commission passes on staff appointments. They are handled in a
pretty perfunctory way."

Even when members have interests in an appointment, their
limited resources and notions about the prerogatives of the chairman
generally serve to mute the assertion of those interests. Late formal
involvement in the process and limited access to information and
expertise provide a weak base for challenging or resisting a recommendation. A generous sense of the role of chairmen and the modest
meaning assigned to the requirement of commission approval diminish
the motivation to challenge. Chairmen are perceived as having special
responsibilities which justify deference to their views. A person close
to the chairmanship of the Civil Aeronautics Board noted, "The Civil

Aeronautics Board is willing to allow the chairman to place his stamp on the personnel of the agency." A former member of the Federal Power Commission explained his willingness to allow considerable latitude to chairmen in this way: "He is the guy who draws the heat, so let him pick." In the Federal Communications Commission, according to a former member, "the commission is usually prepared to accept the chairman's views. They carry great weight. He has to take the heat if things go wrong." He went on to say that there were instances in his experience in which the majority probably had doubts about an appointment, but they went along.[9] A chairman of the commission who served during that period substantially agreed with the assessment, at the same time noting, sourly, "They snap at your heels on particular appointments."

The environment in which major Securities and Exchange Commission appointments are made differs to a degree and is characterized by a rather significant engagement of commissioners in selection processes. The chairman's role remains of great importance, but it is played within the context of highly intimate relationships among staff and commission members and an acute institutional concern for the quality of appointments.[10] The continuous presence of former staff members on the commission during the period examined has accentuated the importance of these contextural elements. Longtime associations and an almost egalitarian quality in staff-member relationships provide commissioners with opportunities to develop informed judgments about the relative strengths and limitations of large numbers of staff members. In comparison with other agencies, there is a broader and more meaningful pattern of consultation in appointments in which weight is accorded the views of members. Chairmen, nevertheless, have extensive discretion in appointment processes.[11]

Regulatory agency chairmen differ in the extent of their personal involvement in top-level appointments, but for many this is a major priority.[12] Chairmen also differ in the extent to which they involve colleagues and the effects that are allowed to result from that involvement. Accommodations to the views of colleagues may be made, depending upon the insistence of those with views, a chairman's sense of the importance of a particular appointment, and the strength of his interest in a candidate. Instances were reported in which a chairman acceded to the preferences of others and made that preference his choice. Accommodation in appointments may add to a chairman's capacity to influence decisions which he considers to be more important. The dynamics were described by a former chairman. Shortly after he took office, a member with whom he had rather large philosophical differences vigorously pushed a close associate for a top staff position. In the face of this strong support, the candidate's basic qualifications, and the absence of more attractive alternatives, the appointment was made, albeit with some trepidation. In gratitude, the commissioner-sponsor indicated on more than one occasion that if the chairman ever needed his support, he would be there, regardless. The appointment was not made to buy influence, but it had that result. Withdrawal, bargaining, and other types of behavior of chairmen that would suggest limitations on their discretion in appointments are quite uncharacteristic, however.

What are the consequences of the impressive role of chairmen in the appointment of key staff officials and, specifically, to what extent can chairmen affect the collective character of the top staff echelon through appointments? There are three aspects of the problem. The first concerns the extent to which chairmen may induce vacancies in order to place persons of their own choosing in critical positions. The second concerns the frequency of opportunities to fill positions, whether induced or not. The third concerns the resulting implications for the general influence of chairmen in agency operations.

When Earl Kintner became chairman of the Federal Trade Commission in 1957, he attempted a series of changes in bureau directorships. He was rebuffed by the other members. Kintner was able to overcome the consequences of their resistance, at least in part, by creating associate bureau director positions and installing in them men in whom he had particular confidence. As the position of chairman has developed there and in other agencies, there is reason to conclude that what Kintner sought but could not obtain is now allowed chairmen as a matter of course. According to a long-time observer of Federal Trade Commission operations, "Chairmen are considered to have the right to bring their own bureau chiefs in." Former Securities and Exchange Commission chairman William Cary, upon becoming chairman in 1961, "got rid of" high-level staff members his predecessor had said were "forced" on him, apparently by the White House. Cary went on to say, "I think it was probably understood . . . when I arrived the heads of divisions would feel their office might be—their status might be subject to change."[13]

The inclusion of substantial numbers of regulatory staff positions in the noncareer executive assignment (NEA) system is important for the opportunities of chairmen to place their own selections in critical positions. NEA positions are in the GS-16, GS-17, and GS-18 range and, according to Civil Service Commission regulations, persons in them: (1) are "deeply involved in the advocacy of Administration programs and the support of their controversial aspects"; (2) "participate significantly in the determination of major political policies of the Administration"; or (3) "serve principally as personal assistant to or adviser of a Presidential appointee or other key political figure."[14]

It is reasonable to infer that in regulatory commissions, the special needs and relationships which justify an NEA designation involve the staff position and the chairmanship. Regardless of whether this is the formal rationale, operationally it would seem inevitable. NEA designation also reflects and reinforces the prerogatives of the chair in the appointment process and the ability of chairmen to make changes in these positions as political or personal considerations dictate. With new chairmen, new staff in key positions might be expected. Overall, the extent to which staff positions are found in the NEA system should be an important indication of a chairman's capacity to shape the nature of staff leadership.[15]

Table 3 lists the NEA positions found in the seven agencies in 1968 and 1972.[16]

TABLE 3
NEA POSITIONS: 1968 AND 1972

	1968	1972
CAB	Executive Director General Counsel Director, Bureau of Economics* Director, Bureau of Operating Rights*	Executive Director General Counsel Director, Bureau of Economics* Director, Bureau of Operating Rights* Director, Bureau of International Affairs Special Assistant to the Director, Bureau of Economics
FCC	Executive Director General Counsel Chief Engineer	Executive Director General Counsel Chief Engineer Special Assistant to the Chairman Chief, Broadcast Bureau Deputy Chief, Broadcast Bureau Chief, Cable Television Bureau
FMC	Managing Director General Counsel	Managing Director General Counsel Confidential Assistant to the Chairman

*Other titles used for NEA designation purposes.

TABLE 3 *(Continued)*

	1968	1972
FPC	Executive Director	Executive Director
	General Counsel	General Counsel
	Chief, Bureau of Power	Chief, Bureau of Power
	Chief, Bureau of Natural Gas	Chief, Bureau of Natural Gas
	Director, Special Projects	—
		Assistant to the Chairman
ICC	Managing Director	Managing Director
	Congressional Liaison Officer	—
SEC	General Counsel	General Counsel
	Chief Accountant	Chief Accountant
	Executive Assistant to the Chairman	—
		Executive Director
FTC	Executive Director	Executive Director
	General Counsel	General Counsel
	Secretary	Secretary
	Director, Bureau of Restraint of Trade	—
	Director, Bureau of Deceptive Practices	—
	Director, Bureau of Field Operations	—
	Director, Bureau of Textiles and Furs	—
	Director, Bureau of Industry Guidance	—
	Director, Bureau of Economics	Director, Bureau of Economics
	Confidential Assistant to the Chairman	—
		Director, Bureau of Consumer Protection
		Director, Bureau of Competition
		Director, Policy Planning and Evaluation

SOURCES: U.S. Senate Committee on Post Office and Civil Service, *United States Government Policy and Supporting Positions,* 90 Cong., 2d sess., 1968; 93 Cong., 1st sess., 1973. (Committee Prints.)

In 1972, the position of executive or managing director was included among the NEA positions in each of the seven agencies. Except for the Interstate Commerce Commission, the general counsel's position was also included. The agencies fall into two basic groups regarding the treatment of the positions heading major line units. One group consists of the Federal Maritime Commission, the Interstate Commerce Commission, and the Securities and Exchange Commission, in which none carry an NEA designation. In the second group, a number of such positions are of the NEA type. In the Federal Power Commission and the Federal Trade Commission, all are NEA except for the top position in the Office of Economics in the Federal Power Commission, a major unit but not a bureau. In the Civil Aeronautics Board, the exclusions are the directorships of the Bureau of Enforcement and the Bureau of Accounts and Statistics. In the Federal Communications Commission, heads of the Common Carrier Bureau, the Safety and Special Radio Services Bureau, and the Field Engineering Bureau are excluded.

There are some differences to be noted between NEA designations in 1968 and 1972, although there were no changes in the number of positions covered in the Federal Power Commission or the Securities and Exchange Commission. There was a decrease in the Federal Trade Commission as a result of a reorganization which reduced the number of bureaus, and in the Interstate Commerce Commission. But there were increases in NEA positions from four to six in the Civil Aeronautics Board, from three to seven in the Federal Commerce Commission, and from two to three in the Federal Maritime Commission.

It is not clear why there is extensive use of the NEA device in some agencies and limited use in others. One may speculate, however, about limited usage in the Federal Maritime Commission, the Interstate Commerce Commission, and the Securities and Exchange Commission. Institutional characteristics which bear directly on the chairmanship may be pertinent. In the Federal Maritime Commission, the potent authority of the chairman may reduce a need for advantages that come with NEA designation. In the Interstate Commerce Commission, likely factors are the relative youth of the reformed chairmanship and continuing sensitivities regarding its emergence. A traditional, deep-seated antagonism to anything that hints at politicalization of the staff is involved in both the Interstate Commerce Commission and the Securities and Exchange Commission.

For the rest, the tendency in recent years has been to extend NEA classification to include the entire top staff tier. Extension in the Federal Communications Commission is particularly interesting, perhaps indicating basic changes underway in the chairmanship. Of greatest importance for now, however, is that so many critical positions in the agencies are linked to the chairmanship in a relationship which implies an ability of chairmen to place people of their own selection in them.

NEA designations only suggest a potential for shaping the composition of top agency staff. An examination of the induced and natural opportunities of chairmen to make top staff appointments will indicate the extent to which the potential is realized. Table 4 shows the number of key positions filled by each chairman serving during the 1961–72 period, starting with the appointees of President John F. Kennedy. The positions included are executive or managing director, general counsel, chief engineer or accountant, and the directorships of bureaus or of divisions and offices of comparable significance. In almost every instance, the number of appointments exceeds the number of positions filled, because some positions were filled more than once. A few actions involved reappointments after reorganizations. They were, in fact, continuations, but there was an act of discretion on the part of chairmen; changes were possible. These appointments are included in the number of positions filled, and the number of continuations is indicated in parenthesis.

Chairmen encounter extensive appointment opportunities during their incumbency, opportunities not limited to NEA positions by any means. The opportunities are greatest during transitions from one administration to another. There often is a wholesale restaffing, or something quite close to it. The process of bringing new people into top-level staff positions is facilitated during transitions by agency reorganizations which tend to come at these times, a matter to be explored in the following chapter. The Federal Trade Commission presents a particularly striking picture of transitional changes. In a relatively brief period after Paul Rand Dixon became chairman in 1961, eight major positions were filled. After 1969, new appointments were made to each of the five major positions remaining after reorganization. Appointments to all save one or two key positions were made in the Civil Aeronautics Board and the Federal Power Commission in the 1961 and 1969 transition periods and in the Securities and Exchange Commission after 1961.[17] Changes were less extensive in the Federal Communications Commission after both 1961 and 1969 and in the Federal Maritime Commission after 1969. George Stafford, who became the permanent chairman of the Interstate Commerce Commission in 1969, filled five positions between then and 1972, but the opportunities were spread rather than concentrated. The most glaring exception to the tendency for extensive alterations during transitions is to be found in the Securities and Exchange Commission during the chairmanship of Hamer Budge

TABLE 4

Appointments to Key Positions: 1961–72

Chairman and Year of Appointment	Number of Positions*	Number of Positions Filled
CAB		
Alan Boyd (1961)	7	6
Charles Murphy (1965)	8	4
John Crooker (1968)	8	1
Secor Browne (1969)	7	6
FCC		
Newton Minow (1961)	7	4
E. William Henry (1963)	7	3
Rosel Hyde (1966)	7	4
Dean Burch (1969)	8	5
FMC		
Thomas Stakem (1961)	8	8
John Harllee (1962)	9	6
Helen Bentley (1969)	7	4 (2)[†]
FPC		
Joseph Swidler (1961)	6	5
Lee White (1966)	6	2
John Nassikas (1969)	7	5
FTC		
Paul Rand Dixon (1961)	8	8 (1)
Caspar Weinberger / Miles Kirkpatrick (1969)	5	5
ICC		
George Stafford (1969)	8	5
SEC		
William Cary (1961)	5	4
Manuel Cohen (1964)	5	2
Hamer Budge (1969)	5	1
William Casey (1971)	10	9 (2)[‡]

*Variations due to organizational changes.
[†]Parentheses indicate number of continuations.
[‡]Extends into 1973.

from 1969 to early 1971. During this period only one appointment was made. The extensive changes came with the next chairman, William Casey.

The staffing activity of chairmen who come into office with a

new administration after an election not only tends to be substantial,
it tends to be concentrated in the early months. Chairmen who follow or who are associated with presidential succession after death or
resignation generally have fewer appointment opportunities, but these
also tend to come shortly after they assume the position. Charles
Murphy's appointments as chairman of the Civil Aeronautics Board
were made soon after his arrival. The same was true for chairmen E.
William Henry and Rosel Hyde in the Federal Communications Commission, Lee White in the Federal Power Commission, and Manuel
Cohen in the Securities and Exchange Commission. The major exception was John Harllee in the Federal Maritime Commission, where the
actions were spread over a longer period.

There is a marked tendency for top staff members to assume a
position with a chairman, then leave with him, especially when the
chairman is involved in a governmental transition.[18] Executive directors and general counsels are most closely associated with chairmen.
During the 1961 and 1969 transitions, occupants of these positions
changed with the chairmanship in all but two instances. The exceptions were the continuation of the Federal Maritime Commission's
general counsel after 1969 and the Federal Power Commission's executive director after 1961.[19] As to the chairmen appointed at other
times, Charles Murphy of the Civil Aeronautics Board had opportunities to appoint new persons to both positions rather soon after taking
office. One or the other of the positions was filled by Henry and
Hyde of the Federal Communications Commission and Cohen and
Casey of the Securities and Exchange Commission.

A cursory examination of the backgrounds of top agency staff
members suggests some constraints on chairmen in the appointment
process, despite their extensive selection opportunities. Most of the
appointees to the positions under examination came from within the
agencies. Chairmen often find themselves filling positions from within because the necessary technical expertise is not readily found outside the agency, because the financial incentives are not adequate to
attract outsiders, and because of strong organizational commitments
to allowing career staff members to reach the top of the ladder.
Executive directors and general counsels are most likely to come
from outside, implying once again a close association with chairmen.
Appointments from without generally have been most common in
the Federal Power Commission and, since 1969, in the Federal Trade
Commission. The Civil Aeronautics Board was also notable in this
regard during the chairmanship of Secor Browne in the early 1970s.
The chairmen involved associated recruitment outside the agency
with efforts to make substantial changes in the conduct of regulatory
affairs.

In conclusion, naming persons to fill key staff positions is among the most important decisions made in any organization. In six of the seven agencies, the chairman and staff members responsible to him have and exercise responsibility for personnel decisions in all except a very few areas in which formal participation by the commissions is required. The evidence indicates that chairmen, executive directors, and personnel staffs are not impeded significantly in the exercise of discretion in these matters. The Federal Communications Commission has restricted the chairman to some extent, resulting in the addition of one more step in the personnel action process in a number of instances, cluttering the agenda of the commission, and the periodic intervention of individual commissioners in personnel determinations. Attention to agency personnel policy and solutions of general manpower problems do not appear to be associated with the reservation of authority, however.

Viewing the agencies together, collective interests of commission members in personnel matters are not well developed even when they have a formal role to play. Members are not necessarily disinterested, but the nature of their interests and the central place of the chairman in personnel processes combine to limit the depth and effect of their involvement.

Furthermore, opportunities, often extensive ones, to fill positions tend to come early in a chairman's period of service. A chairman's reservoir of good will is greatest at this time, and there is an inclination on the part of colleagues, perhaps even more pronounced than at later points, to allow leeway. If transitional situations are marked by the presence of a number of new commissioners, as they often are, permissive tendencies may be accentuated. Regardless of the time factor, chairmen have considerable discretion in the selection of top staff officials. This discretion, plus the availability of appointment opportunities, results in a substantial capacity to shape the upper staff levels. The implications of this capacity for the influence of a chairman in substantive matters will be dealt with in chapter 7.

Financial Resources

The second major area of decision concerning agency resources involves the budget—its development and execution. The budgets of regulatory agencies are small and tight. The amounts available and numbers of positions in Fiscal Year 1976 are summarized in Table 5. Appropriations have increased in recent years, yet the increments have not been equal to rising work loads. There have been decreases in employment levels along with an enlargement of responsibilities in many instances, limiting possibilities for budgetary manip-

TABLE 5

AGENCY RESOURCES: FISCAL YEAR 1976

Agency	Expenditure Authority (in millions)	Positions
CAB	$19.4	758
FCC	49.8	2,113
FMC	7.9	319
FPC	35.9	1,398
FTC	45.7	1,634
ICC	49.8	2,182
SEC	47.2	2,024

SOURCE: *The Budget of the United States Government, Fiscal Year 1976. App., 1975.*

ulation.[20] But policy determinations must still be made concerning the relative emphasis to be given various programs and support of special undertakings of policy significance. Decisions may have broad impact, as when the Federal Communications Commission initiates a full-scale investigation of telephone rates,[21] when the Interstate Commerce Commission begins extensive audits of transportation holding companies,[22] and when the Federal Trade Commission institutes a broad investigation of the petroleum industry.[23]

According to those interviewed, under ordinary circumstances the influence of chairmen in agency budgetary processes and in the critical choices made in that context is considerable, and that of their colleagues is quite limited. The special involvement of chairmen in budget preparation is both reason and indication of their preeminence. By and large, the budgets prepared for commission approval prior to submission to the Office of Management and Budget generally are not informed in any important way by directions from commissioners. In contrast, as a former chairman put it, the chairman is the "focal point" for budget preparation. This means, as indicated by another chairman, "Budget proposals are generally prepared in close cooperation with the chairman. And they reflect the general views of the chairman."

Chairmen are involved in budget preparation through their working relationships with executive directors and budget staffs. They are informed continually about the financial situation of the agency and the particulars to be considered in crafting the budget document, including Office of Management and Budget directives. Judgments on critical questions such as how much to request, allocation priorities, and the strategies to be reflected in the shape and tone of the document are the chairman's to make. Some chairmen invest considerable time and effort in the process. With one notable exception, chairmen during the period studied were involved in a critical and organized manner in preparation and assumed that the product was to be considered "theirs" when submitted for commission action.[24]

Commission members may have some say in the preparation process. Staff may work with particular commissioners on points of personal interest, but the impact of members at this stage is usually indirect and comes through staff perceptions of their preferences and likely reactions. If clear preferences are on the record, perhaps developed in previous years' discussions, they may be taken into account. Even when preferences of members are clear, however, they may not prevail. They must be weighed with technical factors and with the preferences of the chairman. When there is conflict, there is no question about whose views will be accorded greater weight.

Formal commission attention to budget proposals is cursory. Individual commissioners ordinarily spend little time in preparing for budget discussions, and commission deliberations are of short duration. On occasion executive directors have held special budget sessions for members to explain the document, to invite reactions, and, in general, to deepen members' participation in the process. The experience usually has been unsatisfactory. According to one who made a concerted effort, "Many of the commissioners did not attend." And those who did participate often indicated their boredom. Failures of this sort reflect a limited interest in budgetary matters and also the view that the budget is the chairman's affair.

Probably the most potent interest shared by commissioners in the various agencies concerns the total to be requested and the securing of all that can be gotten in increased resources. Defensibility of the document before the Office of Management and Budget and the Congress is an important derivative interest. For example, a person close to the Interstate Commerce Commission commented that the commissioners currently tend to "dig into the budget," suggesting an atypical level of engagement. Their particular interests are different, but "all of them want to look good to the Congress." When former members or staff of Congress are on commissions, they are inclined to be particularly concerned with the defensibility of the budget and in contributing their expertise to developing a persuasive document.

Another budgetary interest at times reflected by commissioners is in the allocation of resources among major agency activities. If aggressiveness in the budgetary process is an indication, coherent and intensely-held positions of this type are more the exception than the rule. To the extent they are present, differences among commissioners are to be expected, thus making unlikely successful joint action to change a chairman's budget.

A potential interest which is seldom apparent is in the budget as an instrument which members, collectively, might use to influence the management of agency affairs through the development and articulation of policies and priorities. One recorded effort with such objectives provides entrée into more general consideration of the relative impact of commissions and chairmen in decision-making regarding financial resources.

The effort began in the Federal Trade Commission in the mid-1960s. Prior to that time, the commissioners were involved in the budget process in a most limited way. The four had "almost no impact on the budget." The general desire of some members for greater participation in agency management and some dissatisfaction with allocation patterns sparked concerted efforts to be involved more extensively and deeply in examining budget recommendations and determining the final product. The members most concerned with management matters sought to use the budget to inform themselves about the conduct of work in the agency and to impose their priorities on that work.

The chairman, Paul Rand Dixon, cooperated to an extent, and sessions were arranged in which staff made presentations on projected work and related budget recommendations, followed by extensive discussion at the commission table. As a result, members had "some" impact, according to a close associate of Dixon's. One commissioner concluded, "Unless the chairman is sympathetic, it won't work." And in this case, "In principle, Dixon did not like their participation."[25]

This example suggests the importance of a chairman's process resources in budgetary matters. Dixon allowed his colleagues a forum in which to assert their views, but the process was not changed to the extent that control was lost. Timing is a particularly important process factor in budget considerations at the commission level. Even when limiting participation is not intended, there may be little time for commission consideration prior to deadlines, and, consequently, limited opportunities for exploration and commission-induced change. If a chairman wishes, he can "orchestrate" consideration so as to maximize the chances of his views prevailing. Time considerations, in conjunction with the restraint of some members results, as in the Federal Trade Commission, in deliberations in which commissioners respond to proposals in an "ad hoc" and "top-of-the-head" manner and "do not look at the larger questions."

The Federal Trade Commission example also suggests the advantages of chairmen in information and expertise. After six years of concerted effort to understand the Federal Trade Commission budget process and to make a substantial impact on and through it, a former commissioner capsulated the experience and the consequences by saying, "I don't know to this day how Rand did the budget." The assumptions upon which the budget was put together, the alternatives that were considered, the reasoning processes, and the bases of particular allocations and the total figure remained mysteries.

Overall, the impact of commissioners on agency budgets ranges from the miniscule through the quite limited and peaks at the exceedingly modest. The characterization of the impact of the members of the Federal Communications Commission as being "about as significant as a nit on the ass of a gnat," coming from a person who has been close to the process there may be something of an exaggeration, but the point is made in a vivid manner. Those interviewed were in general agreement on the limited impact of members. A former staff member who observed the budgetary process in the Civil Aeronautics Board under several chairmen concluded, "There is no way a member can have an impact." In the Federal Maritime Commission, where no budgetary authority is reserved to members, their involvement is in the informational sense only, and there are no indications of any effects whatsoever. A former member of the Federal Power Commission who served with several chairmen characterized the role of commissioners in that agency as "limited." One in a position to observe budgetary decision-making in the same agency in recent years described the role as that of a "rubber stamp." Considerably less than major significance is attached to the participation of Interstate Commerce Commission and Securities and Exchange Commission members as well.

If members have an impact, it is likely to result in favorable treatment for agency activities of particular interest to them. As an example, there are indications that Federal Trade Commission members Paul Rand Dixon and Everett MacIntyre successfully sought to add funds beyond those recommended by the chairman for Robinson-Patman-Act enforcement during the early 1970s. Interests of members, especially senior members, of the Federal Communications Commission and the Interstate Commerce Commission have been of some consequence over the years. The effects are limited and in a sense, crude. They do not constitute "fine-tuning" particular segments of the budgets in regard to what, specifically, should be done and how it should be done.

Seniority and the status and expertise that it brings constitute an important resource that commissioners may employ in budget matters when their interests are involved. Another means for influencing budget decisions is suggested by a limited but successful challenge to a chairman which took place in the Federal Power Commission during Joseph S. Swidler's tenure. Some commissioners, and one in particular, felt strongly that members needed additional staff in their offices. The chairman was asked to include funds in his budget for the positions. He refused, explaining, perhaps facetiously, that more staff assistance would only allow members to write more dissents. He indicated that if the commission insisted, he would do all in his power to prevent the funds' availability. A stalemate resulted in which some members were insistent and Swidler was resistant. There seemed no way, realistically, to incorporate a request in the agency's budget over his opposition. Resolution came when one member broke ranks and carried the issue to the appropriations committees of the Congress, where he found a sympathetic response. Funds were appropriated and additional staff members were provided.

The agency in which outside appeals may have been significant consistently over time, and perhaps still are, is the Federal Communications Commission. There, according to a former chairman, certain members felt no obligation to present a common agency front on budgetary requests. If their own initiatives did not carry at the commission level, they were perfectly willing to express separate positions to the Office of Management and Budget and to Congress. Consequently, the chairman refrained from initiating changes in allocations which he thought desirable. He did not want to risk having his proposals undercut in Congress.

Commissioners with strong views and who are willing to carry their disagreement outside, then, may have an impact on the budgetary decisions of chairmen. But strong views are not to be found with great frequency. When they are, as in the Federal Power Commission case, they may well be on small matters and easily satisfied under ordinary circumstances. When they are not satisfied, members will have reasons for not pressing the cause outside the agency. Carrying disagreement beyond the agency is a radical and drastic action in most contexts. There are risks of embarrassment and loss of good will of the chairman and perhaps that of other members, with serious consequences for a capacity to influence a range of decisions. Beyond the calculus of gains and losses, the implications of violating generally accepted norms of behavior must be considered. In the various commissions there are powerful tendencies to submerge individual differences and to shield them from outside view when the vital interests of the agency are at stake. The magnitude of the resources available to an agency, especially when the financial pinch is being felt, is of fundamental institutional interest. Consequently, most commissioners are inclined to put aside internal differences and to unite before the Office of Management and Budget and the Congress in the assertion of the resource needs of the agency.

Execution is another budget aspect of significance in assessing the relative influence of chairmen and members. There is little room to change spending priorities significantly in the course of the fiscal year. Some adjustments, or reallocations, are always required, however. In these and in fiscal management in the broad sense, chairmen, again, have the dominant role.

Budgetary adjustments with policy significance range from shifting funds for a small number of personnel from one unit to another to, more rarely, the assignment of several hundred thousands of dollars to support an entirely new initiative. Actions in the former category are much more common than those in the latter, of course, although large-scale changes are known to occur. For example, recently a chairman had an executive director "scrape up" approximately three-quarters of a million dollars to support a major policy study. Decisions regarding adjustments even of this magnitude seem to fall almost exclusively within the domain of chairmen in part because of their control over processes. It is not the practice to seek commission approval for alterations. Even sizable adjustments may be made without the prior knowledge of other commissioners.

The Federal Trade Commission is now an exception in part. It recently has established procedures for mid-year program review that involve commissioners in program assessment and changes in allocations. The procedures are part of a larger effort to plan the agency's work program and to assign resources on the basis of meaningful priorities. In the 1975 review, the commission reduced funds allocated to fourteen agency programs, increased allocations to seventeen, and left thirty-one unchanged.[26]

As in personnel decision-making, the limited engagement of commission members in budget matters should not be taken to indicate that their participation is always unwanted or that efforts to limit their participation are normal. Chairmen do not always view the budget proposals prepared under their imprimatur as beyond improvement and their colleagues as without contributions to make. The most assertive chairmen have been known to change their stance on the basis of the arguments of colleagues. At times efforts have been made with the support of chairmen to enlarge the involvement of members in systematic ways in order to elicit collective guidance on policy and program priorities which could then be reflected in resource allocations. In addition to the Federal Trade Commission, the notable examples have been the Federal Communications Commission and the Securities and Exchange Commission. The results in all cases have been mixed. Efforts have been impeded by the essential disinterest of some members, the innovativeness of the approach, and, perhaps most importantly, a considerable gulf in perspectives. The gulf is between a regulatory perspective which emphasizes substantive issues and decision-making in particular cases—the adjudicator's orientation—and one which sees the regulatory process in terms of large policy objectives and program priorities—that of the professional manager.

Agency Governance and Organizational Resources

Decisions about personnel and financial resources affect institutional character in general and specific ways and are important means for shaping substantive regulatory activity. They are important aspects of agency governance. In comparative terms, commissioners are probably more engaged and more influential in personnel matters than in budgetary matters. Even there, their influence is modest in relation to that of chairmen. In both areas, the role of agency chairmen stands out in importance. Whether they elect to maximize their influence or not, their capacities are great in contrast to their colleagues'.

5.

Organizational Structure and Processes

A vast number of phenomena fall under the heading of organizational structure and processes ranging from the most general allocations of authority and responsibility among component organizational units to the particulars of administrative routines. Important consequences for regulation are associated with structure and processes and their maintenance or modification. Among them are adaptability on substantive matters, the orientations reflected in decision-making, and the dispatch with which responsibilities are carried out. As with all complex organizations, the regulatory agencies are engaged continuously in making adjustments in structure and processes through formal and informal means. Much of this activity takes place at the staff level, beyond the ken or involvement of commissioners or chairmen.

The major concern of this chapter is not to examine the particulars of agency structure and processes. As the agency governance context suggests, it is to assess the distribution of influence over structure and processes and the relative capacity of chairmen and members to effect changes.

Chairmen and Major Organizational Changes

Periodically regulatory agencies undergo major reorganizations involving the principal operating units. The frequency with which these occur suggests a certain adaptive capacity in the agencies. Moreover, the major changes provide a starting point for ascertaining, at least in general terms, the place and relative influence of chairmen and commissioners in this sphere of agency governance.

Table 6 indicates periods of major organizational change in each of the agencies during the period under examination. Bureau-level alterations include the creation and demise of major line units, or substantial adjustments in the division of responsibilities among them. Extensive alterations are those that affect two or more existing units. Intrabureau alterations are indicated when the numbers reported suggested a major concern with organizational questions. One, two, or three changes within a bureau or bureaus would not be enough for inclusion. This portion of the table, then, has an impressionistic base.

TABLE 6

MAJOR STRUCTURAL CHANGES: 1961–72

Agency	New Chairmen	Bureau-level Alterations		Major Alterations Within Existing Bureau-level Structure
		Extensive	Limited	
CAB	1961, 1965 1968, 1969	1961	1965	1969
FCC	1961, 1963 1966, 1969		1970	1961
FMC	1961, 1962 1969	1961* 1970	1964 1965 1966 1967	
FPC	1961, 1966 1969	1961		1969
FTC	1961, 1969 1970	1961 1970		1967
ICC	1969†	1965		
SEC	1961, 1964 1969, 1971	1971		1961

*Time of creation out of the Federal Maritime Board.
†Prior to 1969, the chairmanship rotated among members each year.
SOURCES: Annual reports of the agencies.

Intricate structural adjustments occur over periods of time, and the periods may not be encompassed in one year's calendar. The years noted in table 6 accurately indicate the central points of major activity, although the planning and execution of the changes may not have fallen solely within them.

The timing of major structural revisions is closely associated with the arrival of new chairmen during times of governmental transition after elections. In six of the eight instances in which bureau-level organization was reworked thoroughly, both conditions were present. The exceptions are the Interstate Commerce Commission and the Securities and Exchange Commission reorganizations in 1965 and 1971. Limited bureau-level alterations and extensive changes within bureaus show a similar relationship to changes in the chairmanship. The exceptions are the limited bureau-level alterations in the Civil Aeronautics Board in 1965, in which the adjustments were more closely associated with his predecessor than with Charles Murphy, who became chairman that year, and in the Federal Maritime Commission and Federal Trade Commission in the 1966–67 period.

An apparently instinctive urge to reorganize regulatory agencies when administrations change and the policy and program purposes of chairmen complement one another in provoking organizational revisions at such times. New administrations, especially those arriving via election, come to power with a sense of regulatory problems informed by party orientations on economic questions and stimulated by the interests to which they are sensitive. When party control changes in transitions, the pressures are that much stronger. Under such circumstances, built-up criticisms of particular agencies may be transformed from complaints to foundations for action. Reorganizations are major means for taking corrective steps. Those that came after the Kennedy administration assumed power can be traced to various critical assessments of the agencies during the last portion of the Eisenhower years and the statement of deficiencies and recommendations in Dean Landis's report to President-elect Kennedy. Landis's comments on organizational problems were general in nature; major emphasis was on other matters. Although blueprints for structural change were not supplied, the substantial reorganizations which soon came were pointed at the problems he emphasized and were part and parcel of a general revitalization which his analysis was intended to spark.

The regulatory agencies were somewhat less but still the objects of critical attention at the close of the Johnson administration. The 1969 transition to the Nixon administration was not marked by an immediate, systematic critique which defined themes and directions for adjustment. It was two years before a comprehensive statement appeared in the form of the Ash council report. In the meantime, attention focused on the particular problems of some of the agencies, initially the Federal Trade Commission and the Federal Maritime Commission, then later the Federal Communications Commission and the Securities and Exchange Commission. Significant organizational changes were made, or at least considered, as a result.[1]

Although the climate at transition time is favorable to organizational change, alterations must substantially be devised and, of course, implemented within the agencies themselves. New chairmen, the agents of a new administration, generally share a sense of obligation to represent that administration's interests and to correct regulatory errors. Kennedy appointees saw themselves as "reform" chairmen, as did the Nixon appointees. Reorganization is an obvious means for beginning the process of reform. It is also a means to serve several intertwined strategic interests of chairmen. The initiation of structural change thaws established arrangements within agencies. Options regarding how programs will be carried out and, most importantly, who will carry them out are presented. Appointment opportunities are created. Overall, reorganization allows chairmen to press their mark on the agencies in a variety of ways and to underscore the centrality of their position. Thus it is closely associated with the interests of chairmen in agency governance.

The extent and nature of organizational changes depend heavily on the views of chairmen. The choice may be to do much or to do little. For example, despite the general climate and the wave of reorganizations in regulatory agencies in 1961 and 1962, Newton Minow, after considering possibilities for the Federal Communications Commission, elected not to tinker extensively with the agency's structure. The position of executive director was established, but further alterations were not pressed. Minow concluded that, because of the views of several of his colleagues, further initiatives would weaken his influence in substantive areas.[2]

Organizational adjustments are often preceded by studies and recommendations of outside agents, such as the Office of Management and Budget (and its predecessor) and private consulting firms. The views of chairmen are generally taken into account, if not accorded considerable weight.[3] Between recommendation and action, chairmen play an important role in determining what will be done. In a real sense, the major organizational plans that are implemented are those of chairmen, assisted by staff closely linked to them, even when there has been outside assistance.

Other commissioners are engaged in limited ways even in major reorganizations. As in so many areas, their interests are restricted and their involvement comes after proposals have been developed. The effects of their involvement have been modest. Only one instance was discovered in which a chairman, in a sense, lost in a major reorganization effort as a result of the opposition of members. That exception, to be discussed in some detail subsequently, was in the Federal Communications Commission. The lack of enthusiasm demonstrated by the chairman himself at a critical point raises uncertainties about whether the commission's negative reaction should be counted as a complete rebuff.

Modest Proposals

Changes in agency structure and processes ordinarily are much more modest than the extensive reorganizations that have been discussed. Limited adjustments may be quite important individually, however, and over time their collective significance may be of large proportions. Consider, for example, several made in the Civil Aeronautics Board between 1970 and 1972.

1. The financial, personnel, and management analysis functions were brought together under the supervision of the assistant executive director, a new position.

2. A division of the Bureau of Economics dealing with rates was renamed and completely restructured.

3. An office dealing with consumer affairs was created.

4. The Bureau of Enforcement's legal division was split into two parts, with one responsible for formal proceedings and the other for informal compliance.

5. There were structural adjustments at the division level within the general counsel's office.

6. One of the four divisions in the Bureau of Accounts and Statistics was abolished, and its functions were divided among two of those remaining.

7. The positions of executive director and secretary were combined into the position of managing director/secretary to centralize control over staff functions.

8. A long-range planning unit, responsible to the board through the managing director, was created.

9. There were extensive organizational changes within the Bureau of Economics.[4]

Several of the changes clearly were of significance in and of themselves, such as those enhancing the representation of consumer interests and establishing a planning unit. The reorganization of the enforcement function to recognize compliance through informal means reflects significant preferences in regulatory style. The several changes toward more centralized control of staff operations through offices tied closely to the chairman are of basic importance.

As in the case of major reorganizations, chairmen may play an important role in more modest structural changes, adjustments in agency processes, and alterations in the techniques of regulatory program administration. At times they display much interest in such matters. An examination of alterations with which chairmen have been closely identified indicates three sometimes interrelated interests that may prompt personal attention: meeting criticisms that seem politically threatening to the agency, alleviating major administrative problems, and adding to the capacity of the chairmanship to deal with the demands placed upon it.

Examples of changes in structure, processes, and administrative techniques associated with particular chairmen are relatively plentiful. Secor Browne pushed the establishment of a consumer affairs office in the Civil Aeronautics Board in the 1970s. Recent chairmen of the Federal Power Commission and the Federal Maritime Commission sponsored new offices focusing on environmental matters in the first instance and energy matters in the second. George Stafford brought the unit responsible for freight-car availability under his immediate supervision while chairman of the Interstate Commerce Commission. This move, like others mentioned, touched upon a matter of considerable political sensitivity and underscored the efforts of chairmen and their agencies to respond to criticisms.

The one organizational innovation most closely and commonly identified with chairmen in recent years has been the establishment of offices concerned with policy planning and analysis. Among other uses, such offices improve the ability of agencies to deal with criticism and the ability of chairmen to direct agency activity. The names and emphases of the various units differ, but an organizational focus for planning and analysis now exists in most of the agencies.

Several chairmen have pushed the development of data-processing capabilities and computer-based management information and control systems. Process changes associated with chairmen range from rather broad efforts to alter the character of agency operations through, for example, seeking greater "openness,"[5] to altering the way in which particular decisions are made,[6] to introducing innovations in formal case procedures.[7]

The truth of the matter probably is that the personal interests and energies of chairmen account for a small portion of the modest adjustments. Their role is likely to be secondary, though still significant, with the primary actors found at the staff level, especially among executive directors and their associates. That is the level at which problems are identified and courses of action framed. The characteristic role of the chairman is a supportive and legitimizing one. To illustrate, a Civil Aeronautics Board managing director once developed and implemented a rather sophisticated management control system, with a chart room for displaying relevant data and analysis and with periodic briefings for top staff and board members. The initiative for devising the system came from the managing director, not from the chairman, although it was sanctioned and supported by him. The system was evaluated when a new chairman and a new managing director came to the board. The latter concluded that certain aspects of the system, such as the chart room and the briefings, were not useful. Board members, as in other efforts to enlarge their grasp of agency operations, seemed quite "bored" with it all. His views were set out in a memorandum to the new chairman, concluding that unless there was objection, he would terminate those aspects of the system which seemed nonproductive. The chairman provided no objection, and the alterations were made.

Another managing director described a number of "demonstration" changes which he conceived and instituted as part of a general effort to improve the use of agency resources. One change was to employ teams for the periodic inspection of field operations, with the teams consisting of staff drawn from the GS-12 and GS-13 grades. The purposes of the program were to employ the perspectives of a variety of specializations in field inspections and to contribute to the managerial development of those making up the teams. A second change pertained to the investigative activities of the agencies. Structural and procedural alterations were made to ensure that investigations moved on a basis of priorities established by the commission, and that once instituted, they were concluded in a timely manner. One specific step was to break down the insularity of the agency's two major investigative staffs by combining them. A third change concerned program evaluation. A demonstration effort was instituted in one bureau, involving the establishment of realistic goals for auditing accounts of regulated firms and the use of quality controls in the auditing process. These three not inconsequential initiatives were generated at the staff level, but they were discussed extensively with the chairman prior to implementation, because they involved important "conceptual" changes. In addition to securing the approval of the chairman, the discussions were intended to provide him with specific information with which to respond to questions that might be raised by members of Congress or by other commissioners.

Particular adjustments to structure and other aspects of regulation may or may not be presented for commission approval. It is not always clear whether commission consideration is required. The chairman's judgment is often controlling on the point and on the extent of consultation, if any, that will precede implementation. From time to time, there are conflicts. In one fairly recent case, some members viewed an action of the chairman as doing away with a regional office, a matter which they saw as requiring their approval. The chairman's position was that the office had not been abolished but merely downgraded to field office status, something that he could do. Overt conflicts of this type are rare, however.

When matters are brought to the members for approval, that approval is generally forthcoming in routine fashion. In the illustration given above, the commission learned of the chairman's intentions when he announced the appointment to head the new field office. One of his colleagues said, in effect, "Wait a minute. You have the authority to appoint the man, but you don't have the authority to establish the office. We have to do that." After a brief but heated discussion about who had the authority to do what, the chairman said, "All right. I move the establishment of the office." His colleagues promptly and unanimously approved the step.

An exception of sorts to the general deference of members to chairmen in these matters must be entered once again for the Federal Communications Commission. The record indicates a wariness on the part of the members that often takes the form of putting off making any decision at all on a matter brought to their attention. In the Interstate Commerce Commission, the other agency where the chairmanship may be a bit vulnerable, there have been practically no instances since 1969 in which an initiative sponsored by the chairman has been rejected. There are indications that the prospect of controversy may have resulted in some restraint on the part of the chairman from time to time, however. The more characteristic situation is that indicated by one chairman in describing his discussions with senior colleagues on ideas for improving agency operations. At times he was told "Well, that was tried once before, and it didn't work." But, in his view, this was just "friendly advice." If, despite experience, he concluded that the results might be different in present circumstances and with new people, "then they say, O.K."

Even when chairmen and staff conclude that formal commission approval of limited changes is not required, there may be informal consultation. In the case of the demonstration changes which were described, discussions took place with individual members. A strong chance remains that commissioners will not learn about adjustments of this type until after implementation, if at all. A commissioner who served with two chairmen, one highly and the other moderately inclined to consult their colleagues, emphasized the point. In his experience, changes often came to the attention of the commission in accidental ways, revealed in a passing comment of a staff member in a commission meeting.

Recent Cases

Recent experiences in the Federal Communications Commission, the Federal Trade Commission, and the Securities and Exchange

Commission provide additional insights into the relationship between chairmen and commissioners regarding alterations in organizational structure and processes. There were extensive reorganizations in the Federal Trade Commission and the Securities and Exchange Commission in the early 1970s, and a substantial effort was made in the Federal Communications Commission.

The stimuli for reorganization of the Federal Trade Commission were the internal conflicts which had marked the commission during previous years and charges of poor performance. A new administration and a new chairman were the instruments. The analysis and recommendations of a special study group of the American Bar Association and of an Office of Management and Budget group identified specific problems and remedies.[8] Ultimately, the bureau structure of the agency was completely redone, with the number of bureaus reduced from five to three. Another major change was the creation of an Office of Policy Planning and Evaluation.[9] The restructuring took place during the nine-month chairmanship of Caspar W. Weinberger, which began in 1969, and occupied considerable time. One of his major objectives as chairman was to restore harmony to the commission, no small task since former chairman Dixon and two of his major antagonists remained as members. The interaction of the chairman and commissioners on organizational problems took place within the context of Weinberger's general efforts at reestablishing cohesion and effective working relationships.

Specific organizational proposals were shaped by Weinberger and his staff out of ideas contained in the ABA and OMB studies and notions that were generated internally. During the development process, Weinberger invited the suggestions of his colleagues. Although in a real sense the final plan was his, its adoption was preceded by much informal spadework and consultation with other members. Apparently, commissioners Dixon and MacIntyre gave the chairman a blank check regarding particulars; they indicated they would support whatever Weinberger wished to do. Commissioners Philip Elman and Mary Gardner Jones made substantive suggestions which were accepted or rejected by Weinberger after discussion. There was no serious conflict in the process. Instead, there was an apparent general willingness to follow the leadership of the chairman in the matter.

Another major and successful effort at reorganization in which similar inclinations were evident took place at the Securities and Exchange Commission during the chairmanship of William Casey. When Casey became chairman in 1971, he found the Securities and Exchange Commission "dead in the water." There are indications that he was selected for the position because he could get the agency moving once more. The first major reorganization in thirty years was a key part of the invigoration effort. The number of divisions was increased from three to five. Two new divisions focusing on enforcement and market regulation were created through splitting the Division of Trading and Markets. Another new division to focus on investment company regulation was spun off the Division of Corporate Regulation. Investment company disclosure matters were transferred to the Division of Corporation Finance, and all enforcement activities were concentrated in the Division of Enforcement. The position of executive director, which had been abolished in 1961, was reestablished with responsibility for providing administrative and management direction.[10]

The reorganization plan was developed on the basis of assessments made by William Casey and his staff. Other commissioners apparently were not involved at this stage. Ultimately, there was consultation when the chairman "put forward specific propositions and how to do it." According to a member, "By and large, the Commission came into agreement with his proposals and program. They welcomed them. Somebody has to take the initiative in such matters, and it is appropriate for the chairman to do so."

At the time these structural changes were underway, a related analysis of management processes was being prepared by the Office of Management and Budget. Its report recommended a number of improvements. A need for more staff was noted. The basic problems identified in the study concerned the general ways in which work was managed in the agency. They were seen as resulting from an institutional proclivity to control matters on a case-to-case basis, rather than in program management terms. The report stated:

> The organization which has evolved to do this work stresses a legalistic handling of each case utilizing many trained attorneys in key positions and subjecting the case to numerous levels of painstaking review. Relatively little authority is delegated. The stress is often more strongly placed on case development and due process than it is on development and pursuit of program and policy goals.[11]

Furthermore:

> Programs and policy must often be deduced from the emerging body of cases and their disposition other than from a fully articulated written statement of programs, goals, policy, systematic procedures, or operating guidelines.[12]

The major objectives of the suggested changes were to enhance policy-making capabilities at the commission level and to establish a focal point for managerial control in the executive director's office. In regard to the first objective, the critical role of the chairman in policy-making was implied. Certain commission-level staff units were to continue to report directly to him. These included the offices of the general counsel, secretary, administrative law judges, and opinions and review. A number of new units were also to report to him. These included a policy research operation, an office of public information, and an internal audit staff.[13]

Management control over agency operations was to be placed in the executive director, subject to policy guidelines of the commission and exercised through authority delegated by the chairman. Assisted by various staff instrumentalities employing modern management concepts and tools, the executive director was to see that commission policies and priorities were the basis for regulatory activity. He would, in effect, be responsible for the day-to-day management of agency affairs and the direction of divisions and offices.[14] Another set of recommendations concerned particular management problems, such as effectiveness at operating levels, workload imbalances, lengthy processing times, and high turnover in the ranks of attorneys.[15]

Chairman Casey initiated the Office of Management and Budget exploration, although commission approval for the study was obtained. A member of the commission at the time implied that he and his colleagues were restrained in their enthusiasm for the study. They made "no objection" to Office of Management and Budget "taking a look." Their expectations regarding the project were, however, quite modest. Noting that "in theory" the Office of Management and Budget personnel were management experts, it was concluded that some possibly useful ideas might emerge. The more important reason for supporting the study was that "It might educate them [OMB] as to the Securities and Exchange Commission's problems and make them more sympathetic to our budget requests."

Apparently, Casey had developed some rather precise notions about the changes that he wanted to make beyond the reorganization previously described. His independent evaluations reportedly were compatible with the conclusions of the Office of Management and Budget study. His largest interest was in developing a capacity for management control that would allow those centrally responsible, especially the chairman, to shape and reshape those operations as the situation required. Immediate problems, such as work-load imbalances, were of secondary importance.

A number of the specific recommendations which emerged from the Office of Management and Budget study were melded into the package of structural changes developed within the agency. They included the reinstitution of the position of executive director and the creation of a public information office, changes which were put into effect.

It is more difficult to track the impact of the basic concepts and emphases of the Office of Management and Budget report, especially those concerning program management. To attempt to do so requires some discussion of the way the report was handled after completion. It was presented to the commission independently of the major proposals for structural revision. At one point Casey was said to have told the commission that "he thought it was within his power to make changes suggested by the report, but that he would not. He would consult." When the report came before the commission, according to one member, Casey was seen by his colleagues as being closely associated with it. He presented its findings to them. His manner of presentation, however, indicated not so much that the particulars should be considered as his proposals, but that there were interesting ideas in the document that deserved consideration.

Commission consideration produced considerable negative reaction, especially to the concept of management control, and most particularly to broad and potent management control to be exercised by the executive director. The commissioner previously quoted said, "Some felt some suggestions tended to downgrade substantive problems to management technique. There always has been a strong feeling that the executive director should not get too far into substantive matters."

Apparently, the commission neither approved nor disapproved the Office of Management and Budget report. Nevertheless, there have been some interesting reflections, albeit in moderated form, of the basic concepts which it asserted. In commenting on the study, the 1972 annual report highlighted the need for additional resources that had been established in it. This was the aspect which generated the most enthusiasm among the commissioners. According to a person close to the situation, "The commissioners were happy about the study because it gave an argument for more money." In other places the annual report reflected a sense of the importance of management control concepts, despite the cool reception which these had received from the commissioners. For example, the document said: "The reestablishment of the position of Executive Director represents the beginning of a management structure designed to provide executive direction and control, alternative program approaches to meet policy goals, and improved operating systems."[16] Among the activities reported for the executive director during the previous year were "the review and appraisal of internal compliance with the Commission's policies, plans and procedures" and the development of a comprehensive management reporting system to provide data regarding "major workload and cost items, significant events, industry operations and progress on rules, regulations, and other Commission projects." Also a reorientation was noted putting the budget to use "as a key management tool in establishing priorities and allocating resources."[17]

Despite indications of change, the executive director of the Securities and Exchange Commission has not emerged as the potent and comprehensive control point envisaged by the Office of Management and Budget study. Yet, in theory and in current manner of operation there is some compatibility with major concepts developed in the recommendations. The position of executive director has become a central position in the processes of the agency, principally as a result of the initiatives of a chairman, and perhaps in spite of reluctance on the part of some commissioners.

In contrast to the Federal Trade Commission and the Securities and Exchange Commission experiences that resulted in changes, the organizational assessment of the Federal Communications Commission had limited impact. The reason was not a clean bill of health. On the contrary, the Office of Management and Budget study found considerable disarray. Management in the agency had a very narrow meaning, essentially referring to housekeeping matters. Supervision, ordinarily the responsibility of officials who considered themselves to be subject-matter specialists first and foremost, tended to be spasmodic rather than systematic. A disdain for and a disinterest in management per se was apparent. According to the report, there was no authoritative management mechanism. Management responsibility was diffused; no one was really in control. Delegation of authority for management action was lacking. The extensive retention of authority for agency management by the commission as contained in Administrative Order Number 11 was identified as a main source of problems. "Thus," the report found, "the seven commissioners have a string of minor and major management issues paraded past them for judgment without adequate time for reflection, sufficient information for insight or any opportunity to plan the managerial edifice they are building a brick at a time."[18] Members indicated to those who did the analysis "that they really don't know what is going on in the staff levels below the bureau and office level. . . ."[19]

As in the case of the Securities and Exchange Commission, the concept of managerial control was fundamental to the major changes which were suggested. The key proposal was to remove administrative responsibility from the commission and to lodge "executive authority" in the chairman, qualified by recognition of the chairman as "one among equals" in quasi-legislative and quasi-judicial matters. Specifically included in the chairman's authority were the selection of key staff, delegation of authority to them, and making "management policy determinations."[20]

The major mechanism for carrying out the management responsibilities of the chairman was a new position, that of general manager, with responsibility to "implement the Chairman's management policy by directing and coordinating the work of the staff." It was specified that the general manager should have no role in substantive determinations except in connection with timeliness and efficiency of decision-making processes.[21]

Other suggested organizational changes included the establishment of a Bureau of Management Services, in which the various support functions would be housed; a Bureau of Technical Policy, Research, and Development, with responsibility for the development of technical concepts and processes to facilitate the work of the commission; and a Bureau of General Radio Services, to assume many of the responsibilities of the Safety and Special Radio Services Bureau, the Field Engineering Bureau, and the Office of the Chief Engineer.[22] The analysis of problems was more extensive than indicated by this summary of some of the major recommendations. But the rather fundamental character of the critique is suggested.

As in the Securities and Exchange Commission, the study in substantial part was initiated by the commission's chairman, then Dean Burch. Unlike William Casey, who had developed his own precise assessment of the Securities and Exchange Commission situation, Burch was stimulated by an "itch" and had no particular agenda of his own for changes. The executive director, who also was instrumental in initiating the study, had some ideas that were close in many ways to the Office of Management and Budget assessment and prescriptions.

The process employed in commission consideration of the report was somewhat disjointed. For a long period of time after completion, it received no formal attention. It was the subject of discussion in the chairman's office, but without conclusive results. Those involved "fiddled back and forth," according to a participant. "There were always more things to do than there was time for. This one would get dropped off." There was little inclination to add the issues raised by the report to the other contentious matters before the commission. The loss of ground on important substantive matters was seen as a risk of pushing on organizational questions.

When consideration began, it was the executive director who carried the matter forward. Three sessions for discussing the report were held. The first involved the executive director and the commission; the second involved the executive director and top-level staff; and the third involved both groups. By the time the sessions were finally scheduled, whatever support for action there might have been had died. Considerable opposition to various aspects of the report surfaced among both staff and commissioners. Some members "rose up" at the prospect of a general manager and apparently expressed their views openly. The chairman's office received complaints from Congress about the "terrible" changes being planned and the "devious power play" by Burch and the executive director "to diminish the authority" of the six other members.

To members of the Federal Communications Commission, the suggested structural changes and alterations in the management responsibilities of the chairman were unacceptable, even when interlaced with statements recognizing the commission's collective primacy in substantive matters and limitations on the role of the general manager. Formal changes along these lines were quashed. The involvement of members and their impact on major proposals were negative and decisive. However, some aspects of the report could be implemented on the authority of the chairman through the executive director without explicit commission approval. Concepts of overall management of the conduct of work from a central point and more rational approaches to resource allocations employing relevant data and a sense of priorities were reflected later in operational adjustments.

The Federal Trade Commission and Securities and Exchange Commission cases illustrate the extensive organizational changes which may result from the initiatives of chairmen, their leadership role in such matters, and the more limited role of colleagues. Members are not always just ciphers, however. Although the lack of success in the Federal Communications Commission was clearly owing in part to the manner in which the Office of Management and Budget recommendations were handled and the failure of the chairman to sponsor them truly, the resistance of commissioners to changes perceived as altering the system of governance obviously was an important factor. Even in the Securities and Exchange Commission, there were limits to the changes which members would accept. As a result, the proponents pulled back on some fronts, or at least they did not press strongly for elements in the Office of Management and Budget study which members questioned. Thus, the influence of chairmen in organizational change is not unqualified, especially when major departures from the familiar are at issue.

The Securities and Exchange Commission and the Federal Communications Commission cases also illustrate the importance of the conceptual and the unique ability of chairmen to institute or allow alterations in concepts regarding regulatory administration regardless of the views of their colleagues. In both instances, the program management orientation of the Office of Management and Budget studies and the biases toward more centralized control through use of modern management techniques came to be reflected in the two agencies in a variety of ways. That reflection is clearer in the Securities and Exchange Commission. More subtle but no less interesting changes began to be apparent in the Federal Communications Commission as well.

Agency Governance and Agency Administration

The central place occupied by chairmen in important decisions about organizational structure and processes is striking, as it was shown to be in the preceding chapter in questions about personnel and financial resources. Particularly, the close association between the arrival and departure of chairmen and structural changes suggests the capacity tied to the position and agency dependency upon the chairmanship for initiating and steering through major adjustments. Considering organizational resources, structure, and processes together, it is clear that a truly broad and significant range of agency concerns falls principally in the domain of chairmen, with important implications for substantive regulatory determinations. The connections may be seen with some clarity through an examination of commission and staff-level relationships in substantive matters.

6.

Chairmen, Commissioners, and Staff Leadership

One of former Federal Communications Commission member Nicholas Johnson's least controversial pronouncements may have been, "It is axiomatic that an administrative agency's staff has substantial power in channeling and influencing the agency's actions."[1] Unquestionably, commission action is affected by the staff. Commission decisions almost without exception are preceded by staff work and are based upon analyses and recommendations of staff associated with the various bureaus and offices. The stakes in staff work include much more than the choices made in particular substantive determinations. Regulatory agendas and priorities are shaped at the staff level and have their largest reflections there. Highly salient manifestations of regulatory style are found in staff activity.[2]

Questions about regulatory agency governance may be answered substantially in terms of influence over staff work. Many regulatory efforts begin and come to a conclusion there. Commissions, realistically, cannot be expected to depart regularly and extensively from decisional foundations and rationales provided by staff. Staff efforts in the form of special studies are particularly vital elements in regulatory processes and are major vehicles for developing policy initiatives and responses.

The assertion that in important matters commissioners are virtual captives of staffs is not uncommon. In this view, "Members work in the area of discretion allowed them by the staff," according to a former staff member and chairman's assistant. A supportive notion emphasizes the distance between agency members and staff, a condition judged to accentuate the staff role. One piece of imagery used to suggest the condition is the fog bank that obscures the view and understanding of commissioners on the one hand and staff on the other.

Questions regarding the relative influence of top-level officials and staffs possessing expertise, a mastery of detail, and continuing and intimate involvement with problems are not restricted to regulatory commissions. Obscuring mists separating those at the top and those at working levels and weighing on agency effectiveness are not uncommon conditions. Organizations headed by single administrators are no less dependent upon staff or subject to organizational dilemmas when there is confusion in the roles of staff and agency heads in making critical choices. The multimember character of the top level in regulatory commissions may be suspected plausibly to accentuate difficulties in staff direction with adverse consequences for the regulatory process. Collective responsibility to some critics implies a weakness in mechanisms for steering staff-level activity, contributing to vague and conflicting policies and priorities, irresponsibility, and ineffectiveness. But the rather large role that has developed for chairmen in the areas examined in previous chapters suggests the possibility of an enlarged role in staff direction. In this chapter, commission-staff relationships will be explored to ascertain the extent to which this is the case.

Prior to focusing directly on questions of influence and leadership it might be useful to discuss the nature of activity at the staff level. Two important distinctions may be applied generally, although the nature of staff activity varies considerably from agency to agency. The first distinction is between mandated and discretionary activity. Mandated activity includes rate, license, and other types of basic proceedings which the agency must handle because of statutory requirements. The precise nature and volume of mandated activity is to a significant extent beyond control, determined instead by the initiatives of the regulated. Mandated activity generally results in decisions made in adjudicatory context which affect one or a few parties. Discretionary staff activity usually takes the form of "studies," a generic term which incorporates various types of inquiry and actions which such efforts precipitate. Many studies are for internal use and are to illuminate problems and to recommend positions or courses of action that will surface later and perhaps indirectly in formal proceedings. Others may result in public stances, legislative positions or proposals, rules, or the initiation of a proceeding, as in an enforcement action.

Typically, a sizable number of studies will be underway in each agency at any given time, with the trend in recent years being larger and larger numbers stimulated by an increased emphasis on rule-making as a means for enunciating policy. In 1972, for example, the Civil Aeronautics Board reported numerous staff studies in process concerning service to small communities, charter operations, restrictions on air taxi operations, freight forwarder practices, and several special route-related matters. Studies also were underway in connection with several board proceedings, including the investigation of air service in New England, the basis for determining subsidies paid to local carriers, and passenger fare structure.[3]

The second distinction is between activities of routine and critical character, a distinction which lies in the conceptual underpinnings of the decisions that result and the degree of change in concepts of regulation that is involved.[4] Many but not all staff activities that may be categorized as discretionary deal with regulatory problems at the conceptual level, asking such questions as the nature of the problem, its importance, the regulatory objectives and orientations which should be brought to bear, and the proper course of action to follow. Many but not all staff activities that may be characterized as mandated are of a routine nature because they deal with regulatory problems on the basis of established conceptual formulations. In the issuance of a license, for example, staff ordinarily is guided by an established concept of licensing which defines the relevant factors, how they should be weighed, and thus whether a license should be awarded. Established conceptual formulations, however, may be questioned in mandated proceedings or the situation may be in some sense "new," causing staff activities to assume a critical quality.

Critical determinations in the context of mandated proceedings may be illustrated by reference once again to the Civil Aeronautics Board. The major mandated proceedings concern rates, routes, service operations, mergers and acquisitions (and other financial control questions), intercorporate agreements, local service subsidies, licensing of services such as freight forwarding, and enforcement. Several obviously involve balancing carrier and consumer interests and competition within the air transportation industry—two aspects of regulation of critical significance. Proceedings may result in conclusions based upon previously established concepts. But they may also serve as a means for reformulating notions of the appropriate balance of consumer and carrier interests and the nature of competition to be encouraged among carriers.

From the perspective of agency governance, three aspects of influence over staff activity, both routine and critical, stand out in importance. The first is influence over the initiation of discretionary staff activity, particularly that which has conceptual significance. The second is influence over the transformation of activities from the routine to the critical category, allowing reexamination of established

conceptual formulations and the possibility of change. The third is
the conceptual possibilities themselves which become involved in
critical staff effort. The principal emphasis of this chapter is on the
extent to which staff activity, especially in its discretionary and
critical dimensions, is subject to commission-level governance and the
relative influence of chairmen and their colleagues in the governance
of that activity.

Overview

Staff activities, especially those of the discretionary type and
having conceptual significance, are influenced substantially from the
commission level. This is not to suggest an absence of the independent
development and articulation of points of view, positions, and proposals by staff. The requirements and spirit of the Administrative
Procedure Act and generally accepted notions associating at least
some staff independence with decisions of high quality are reflected
in organizational climates in significant ways. Staff independence is
stimulated when issues cut across jurisdictional lines as they not infrequently do, drawing the attention of units with different problem
perspectives and competing interests. A clear illustration is in the
Federal Trade Commission where, it has been said, "The Bureau of
Economics likes, maybe, 10 percent of the Bureau of Competition's
cases."[5] Independence and the development of diverse points of view
at the staff level also may be created purposefully through organizational arrangements. The Civil Aeronautics Board's Office of Consumer Advocate is a prime example,[6] as are the increasingly common
policy analysis groups which have been established to provide critical
assessments and alternatives in regulatory processes.[7] Substantial
commission-level influence, then, does not mean domination. But the
general orientations and broad outlines of staff activity are shaped to
a considerable extent from above. The nature of discretionary efforts
and the conceptual elements of staff work are affected in important
ways by commission-level direction and staffs' perceptions of what is
wanted.

Chairmen, members, and staff generally perceive chairmen as
more potent sources of influence over staff activity than other members, individually or collectively. The perceived influence of chairmen justifies describing the chairman's role in leadership terms, as
leader of the staff. Although there is some ambiguity in the contours
of the role, there is a shared sense that it is appropriately different
and special in comparison with that of other members.

In broad terms, the views of chairmen regarding what should be
done and how are highly persuasive for the staff, and the work done

at the staff level and the products often bear the chairman's stamp, especially in matters of policy significance. As one chairman put it, "All commissioners are equal, but the chairman is more equal than others. It is natural that staff will look to the chairman for direction." Another commented that it was "inevitable" that the chairman's positions would carry considerable weight with the staff. A former commissioner, who also had staff experience, noted, "The staff looks to the chairman for guidance and direction." According to a former commissioner of another agency, "the chairman is the dominating factor" for the staff. A long-time staff member of still another agency bluntly asserted, "Bureau people will follow the chairman even when they disagree. A chairman can be as strong as he wishes with the staff. They look there for leadership."

Some qualifications ultimately will need to be entered to these rather strong characterizations. But it is clear that staff are seen to be quite sensitive to the views of chairmen. Not only are ears open to unvarnished expressions, but cues and signals are sought in the tea leaves of the chairman's day-to-day activities, including, for example, public statements, questions asked in meetings, and the character of appointments. One staff member pictured his colleagues as "eager to learn the chairman's feelings on various subjects." A former long-time staffer put it in more earthy terms: "Staff tries to sniff the water concerning the chairman's preferences, and they will respond to them."

Variations in staff leadership by chairmen are to be discerned from agency to agency and from chairmanship to chairmanship. The leadership role of chairmen seems clearest, most secure, and most potent in the Civil Aeronautics Board, the Federal Maritime Commission, the Federal Power Commission, and the Federal Trade Commission. Although the leadership role is substantial, it is less sharply defined and predictable in its effects in the Federal Communications Commission, the Interstate Commerce Commission, and the Securities and Exchange Commission. The expectations of colleagues and staff are not quite as supportive. The tendency of staff to identify with the chairman is not as pronounced. Members of these agencies have more contact with staff. In the Federal Communications Commission, for example, "Some commissioners get around the building and make their views known," and staff members there are inclined to take matters to commissioners. The assignment of continuing responsibilities to members in areas such as spectrum management, telephone, telegraph, and civil defense also encourages interaction with staff.[8] The division structure of the Interstate Commerce Commission has a similar effect. A strong tradition of intimate staff-commissioner contact is present in the Securities and Exchange Com-

mission. Large numbers of staff attend the frequent commission
meetings and work with members in a variety of other ways although
necessities of order have limiting effects. A recent chairman observed
that on more difficult matters commissioners may meet with the
staff. But when this happens, "The chairman hears about it. We try
not to go off in different directions without the others knowing."

Chairmen and their backgrounds, inclinations, objectives, and
working practices are important elements in the particular form
which leadership takes. But the foundations of the leadership role
seem to be in the position of chairman, not in the desires and skills
of incumbents. In the remainder of this chapter, these foundations
and the factors which affect relationships among chairmen, members,
and staff will be explored in some detail, followed by an examination
of working relationships between chairmen and staff and an assessment of the impact which chairmen may have through staff leadership.

Shaping Leadership Patterns

Staff leadership from the commission level is dependent upon the
capacity to transmit views and the receptivity of the staff to those
views. Chairmen overshadow their colleagues on both counts. This
general condition and the particulars of the chairman's leadership
role result from the expectations and interests of chairmen, colleagues,
and staff and from the distribution of knowledge and process resources.

The expectations of chairmen, members, and staff are that there
should be a special relationship between chairmen and staff, and that
providing direction to staff efforts is a central part of the chairman's
job. A former member described, approvingly, the chairman's most
important functions as being to "move the staff along" and to exercise "responsibility for its direction."

Some differences appear when attention turns to the particulars.
Three general perspectives may be distinguished—the administrative,
the representational, and the executive. In the administrative perspective, a moderate amount of substantive direction is sanctioned.
Emphasis is placed on directing staff in order to expedite work and
to secure the timely and comprehensive presentation of materials
necessary for commission decision-making activity. The other perspectives incorporate this view with additions. In the representational
perspective, the chairman is expected to guide staff on behalf of the
commission and on the basis of the views of the commission. He is to
speak for the commission to the staff; he is to function as the agent
of his colleagues. In the third perspective, the executive, the chair-

man is expected to provide leadership based upon his own views and priorities.

The perspectives do not always appear in singular form. Nevertheless, they are useful for highlighting different expectations found among regulators. The administrative perspective is characteristic of some members, but it is almost never expressed by chairmen or staff. The executive perspective is more likely (though not exclusively) to be found among chairmen. The representational perspective seems to be the most commonly held among all three groups. It is often accompanied by an appreciation that as a practical matter, because of the frequent absence of clear positions to represent, the views of chairmen may predominate.

Expectations regarding leadership of the staff must be considered with what chairmen may unquestionably do and what they must unavoidably do in agency operations. Chairmen are provided a core leadership capacity by formal arrangements which both inform general expectations and serve as a means for carrying the role beyond what some colleagues would perhaps wish. The leadership capacity of chairmen is not based simply upon acceptance by colleagues and staff; there are other parts. The relationship between expectations and position is suggested by two recent statements in congressional settings, one by a former member and the other by a sitting member. In testimony supporting the strengthening of the collective role of members in agency management and greater independence, former Federal Trade Commission member Everett MacIntyre noted:

> It should not be overlooked that . . . investigations are carried on and managed by a professional staff of lawyers, economists, and investigators. Since 1950, for all intents and purposes, the management and work of the professional staff of the . . . Commission in the performance of such quasi-legislative functions has been under the direction of a chairman serving at the pleasure of the President and not under the direction of the Commission itself.[9]

In confirmation hearings on his renomination, Interstate Commerce Commission member Robert Gresham was queried by Senator Vance Hartke about his role in directing staff activities. The exchange provides an interesting glimpse of the domain of chairmen and the realities of their continuing relationships with staff, as seen by a member.

> *Senator Hartke:* All right. Now, let's assume that that happens. What can you do to make sure that . . . the order is effectively carried out?
> *Mr. Gresham:* Well, we have—we have some investigators who can check but more than that—
> *Senator Hartke:* How many investigators do you have?
> *Mr. Gresham:* Oh, I guess, all told, maybe a hundred.

Senator Hartke: One hundred, right?

Mr. Gresham: A hundred twenty.

Senator Hartke: Are they working or are they on a summer holiday?

Mr. Gresham: I hope they are working. So far as I know they are working. Those with whom I am acquainted are working.

Senator Hartke: Well, who is in charge of them? Are you?

Mr. Gresham: No sir.

Senator Hartke: Why not?

Mr. Gresham: Well, the chairman has the administrative direction of the commission. No individual commissioner has any responsibility for the direction of the staff on a day-to-day basis. The reorganization—

Senator Hartke: How about a week-to-week basis?

Mr. Gresham: Well, not on any basis. I have a staff of six people and they are responsible to me and I direct their activities.

. . . . .

Senator Hartke: As far as administration is concerned, that is all the authority you have; is that right?

Mr. Gresham: That is true, sir.

. . . . .

Mr. Gresham: He [the chairman] is the chief administrative officer of the Commission and he is responsible for the day-to-day operations of the Commission and I don't stand in judgment on him, but I will say this . . . I think all of us Commissioners could be helpful to Chairman Stafford, in the day-to-day operations of the Commission, and I really am amazed sometimes that he is able to do all the things he does with respect to running an operation as large as ours.

We have some 1,900 employees but the transportation interests and the caseload are so diverse and so divergent that I really am amazed that he is able to do the things he does. But if Chairman Stafford does not choose to delegate any responsibility to the Commission, I am not going to argue with him about it, Mr. Chairman, because if I were Chairman of the Commission, I might do the same thing or I might run it differently, I don't know.[10]

For Commissioner Gresham and other members, an understanding that chairmen must be involved intimately with staff and an appreciation of the inevitable effects of that involvement for the influence of members combine to create a sense of resignation regarding their own staff leadership possibilities.

Chairmen have numerous linkages with staff that allow them "to keep in touch with what is going on," as one put it, and that provide access to key determinations made at the staff level. Several are associated with administrative responsibilities. One very important leadership resource, as described by a chairman, is "to name bureau chiefs who share the philosophy of the chairman." According to a long-time staff member of the Federal Trade Commission who observed a number of chairmen from close quarters, "The power of appointment is the key. Bureau directors will do anything the chairman wants. All he

has to do is to provide a subtle hint."[11] Positions may also be filled
at lower levels with the compatibility of points of view in mind. The
budget process is of obvious importance, especially in connection
with priorities which guide staff work. Overseeing activities for such
benign purposes as expediting them may lead to the exercise of
influence over their substance. Related management processes can be
important means of access. One chairman, for example, received a
report on work progress each month from his executive director. The
report would be returned with "penciled scrawls" indicating the
chairman's wishes on critical matters and put so there was no doubt
about substantive import. This chairman employed a variety of means
for influencing staff activity, but the monthly review of dry statistics
was one of the most significant.

Other aspects of the chairman's role relate more directly to the
content of staff efforts. The office of the chairman is an important
point for the resolution of intra-staff conflict. Mediation of contending positions held by staff members provides an opportunity to affect
the form that resolution will take. Chairmen generally have an important part to play in initiatives concerning important regulatory
problems. Staff studies are a significant element in these initiatives,
preceding commission consideration of policy departures or the institution of proceedings which will have that result. Chairmen have
considerable freedom to initiate staff studies and generally must approve the execution of major studies initiated by others. Consequently they may influence the form, scope, and other features of such
efforts and, at least to an extent, the results. The capacity to "design
exercises" in the chairman's office and "to direct studies carried out
by the staff," to quote two chairmen, are among the more potent
leadership resources available.

The chairman's position as the focal point for the agency's external relationships and his role as spokesman also are means for
influencing staff work. Chairmen must oftentimes interpret demands
and requests of congressional and other interested parties to the staff.
They may become directly involved when staff activity requires
liaison or negotiation with outside elements. Speeches and statements
allow chairmen to articulate a context for staff effort and to stimulate
particular lines of activity.

Receptivity to the leadership of chairmen is generally high among
staff, especially those at the upper levels.[12] They tend to look to
chairmen for direction, whether appointed by them or not. Top staff
view themselves as "the chairman's men" for the most part. Even in
the Federal Communications Commission, according to an assistant
to a recent chairman, "As a general proposition, all the top staff felt
they were working for us." This does not mean that top staff are not

to be the commissions' men in any sense. But in the complex of
relationships, the ties to the chairmanship in most instances are
clearest, strongest, and most significant for what happens at the staff
level. A former Civil Aeronautics Board staff member put it this way:
the bureau heads think of the chairman as the "head of the agency,
as the boss." In the Federal Trade Commission, according to a former
commissioner, key staff officials are "his people." From agency to
agency, similar characterizations emerged from the interviews. Again,
to ensure that there is no misunderstanding, the appellation, "the
chairmen's men," does not suggest total domination by or automatic
compliance with the wishes or whims of chairmen without regard for
commissions. Rather, it means a strong identification with the chairmen as the operating head of the agency.

Staff members do not "sniff the water" just because it is appropriate to do so. The balance struck among tangible interests engaged
in the relationship between staff and chairmen reinforces receptivity.
Upper-level officials may lose by not being responsive. "The top men
in the bureaus are dependent on the good will of the chairman," as a
former occupant of that position put it. Consequently, he continued,
"The chairman can control the work processes at the staff level."
Opposition to a chairman can be costly in personal and organizational
terms. The staff knows that the chairman "can clip their wings."
Wings can be clipped in a variety of ways. Career advancement may
be impeded. The chairman "possesses so much power over a man's
career . . . that it takes a strong man to resist," according to a former
commissioner. A chairman may prevent individuals or organizational
units from participating in matters of importance to them, and he may
deny his "support for staff purposes."[13] Funds and positions may be
increased, or they may not. Staff may be protected from or exposed
to external pressures. Given the various ways in which chairmen may
assist or penalize staff, it is at least understandable that, as a former
commissioner observed, staff members "do not want to fight city
hall."

Perhaps the most significant interest of staff in relationships with
chairmen is simply in having direction to facilitate their efforts. The
chairman is the likeliest source of direction from the commission
level. One close observer asserted that agency staffs "crave direction."
In his experience, whenever there was "a lack of consistent personal
leadership" from the chairman, the staff "chafed"; the provision of
the type of direction which the staff desired was "something only the
chairman can do." That may be putting it a bit strongly. There is
little question, however, that from the staff perspective some direction is functional and desirable. Although it may very well be that
staffs ideally "want leadership from the commission, not from one

man," as another former staff member argued, direction from the collegium often is not forthcoming. Attention, then, inevitably turns to the chairman.

Inability to penetrate the fog bank to views held at the commission level creates uncertainties which can be costly to staff. There is a real risk of "spinning wheels" and of embarrassment when matters find their way to the commission. In explaining what he saw as rather impressive staff responsiveness to the leadership of a chairman, one former assistant analyzed the situation in this way: "They liked the leadership. Previously they had been adrift. They would go to the commission meetings on their own, uncertain as to what the commissioners wanted. So they would make mistakes." A commissioner who previously served for a long period at the staff level observed, "Staff does not want to propose something the chairman won't like—or the commission either, for that matter."

Conflicting direction may be as frustrating as no direction at all. A former staff member, then a commissioner, suggested that staff looks to the chairman to avoid having to contend with five different positions. Another observer saw a favorable inclination toward the chairman's leadership, "because otherwise there are too many signals." A long-time staffer put it most succinctly, saying, "The staff wants one boss." Therefore, even when commissions speak, if they speak in several languages, staff will best understand that spoken by the chairman.

There also may be staff interests in an agency and its institutional well-being that are served by acceptance of the leadership of chairmen. Staff support contributes to strong chairmanships, and strong chairmen tend to enjoy public stature and visibility. "The better the chairman looks, the better they look." Staff likes the "appearance of strength" and the "limelight." Not only are there personal satisfactions derived from association with an agency which is active and whose chairman is highly visible and well-regarded, there are possibilities of associated gains in such areas as the budget and statutory authority.

On the other hand, career personnel have institutional interests which chairmen may appear to threaten. When this is the case, wariness may have a moderating effect on a chairman's capacity for leadership. Among these interests are the orderly development of the legal framework administered by the agency, freedom from partisan policy interference, and, again, the public repute or standing of the agency.

Staff assessments of chairmen—especially as to their capacities and intentions in relation to the interests just mentioned—determine the degree of caution with which chairmen will be received. There are several points to which staffs seem especially sensitive. They expect chairmen to possess expertise in the relevant subject-matter and "an understanding of the field of work"; to accept economic regulation as a legitimate enterprise; to accept the basic outlines of the regulatory framework as it has developed over the years; and to be activists in the context of that framework.[14] Chairmen also are expected not to be narrowly partisan in the execution of their responsibilities.[15] They are expected to maintain harmonious working relationships at the commission level and the appearance of commission support for their efforts, or to prevent severe conflict which would disrupt work below. Finally, chairmen are expected to have "presence," or to look and act like a chairman and to project personality within and without the agency in a way that reflects favorably on it.

Chairmen who come to their positions considered to be novices in the field, cool to the concept of regulation, overly-critical of the agency's past performance, and political in their orientations may overcome what will probably be a marked staff reserve through the manner in which they conduct themselves. A person close to a chairman who came to an agency without an extensive background in that area and with a strong political identification described the initial staff reaction as "being afraid we would do something silly. But when we got beyond that, we could do a lot of business."

The most common source of caution in staff-chairman relationships is one which is present no matter how well chairmen meet the various expectations. It is a well-justified sense of the chairman as "passing through," or as there in a leadership position for only a limited period of time, then to be succeeded by another with perhaps quite different ideas. Caution may color receptivity to the initiatives of chairmen which would require the extensive investment of resources and suspected of not enduring beyond the tenure of their sponsor. Over time, chairmen assuming the position with a flourish and attempting to bring about significant adjustments which are viewed with some trepidation by the staff may overcome initial reluctance. For example, some staff members were reported to have been unsettled by the early initiatives of chairmen Swidler of the Securities and Exchange Commission and Dixon of the Federal Trade Commission during the early 1960s, but their reserve regarding the two chairmen diminished in time.

Initial staff caution or even continuing limited staff receptivity does not mean an absence of influence of chairmen over work at the staff level. The tangible resources of the chair remain to be employed. But the path to desired ends may be more difficult than when staff reacts positively to a chairman. When an unsympathetic staff is presented with the initiatives of a chairman in whom it lacks confidence, its critical capabilities come forth. Questions are raised and negative reactions are given to suggestions of the chairman. In the case of a request for an investigation or study, the staff "may say something is wrong with the request," but in the final analysis they "will not say no to the chairman," according to one who experienced staff reserve. The importance of the authority of position in such circumstances was indicated by a staff member when asked about staff response to a chairman who failed to meet many staff expectations. Receptivity to the chairman's leadership "never took hold below a certain level," the level just beneath that of bureau director. Nevertheless, according to him, "The chairman's will has been imposed."

Whereas chairmen are closely, if not intimately involved with the staff, commissioners tend to be relatively removed from staff activity until matters reach them for formal determination. If they are involved prior to the completion of preparatory staff work, chairmen usually will have had a central part in that involvement, through bringing matters to members for their reaction or shaping commission wishes and articulating these to the staff. In either case, the position of chairman remains critical.

Their comparative isolation removes members from much of regulatory significance, and, to employ a characterization of Federal Maritime Commission members, causes them to be "shut off from facts and intelligence about the industry" and from the expertise of the staff. Isolation is both a consequence and a cause of intimate chairman–staff relationships and thus has significance for the products of staff activity and for decision-making at the commission level, as will be seen in the next chapter.

Some restraints on the involvement of commissioners with staffs are imposed and others originate with members themselves. Imposed restraints have an institutional quality and consequently are difficult for individual members to overcome. The general acceptance of the chairman's special relationship with the staff has a corollary that commissioners should not interfere with that relationship. In the Interstate Commerce Commission, for example, there is a "lot of respect for the authority of the chairman" in relation to the staff. Also, staff members exercise considerable control over relationships with commissioners. A former member, in describing his experience with staff, noted that the working relationships that developed came "more by initiation of the staff" than the other way around. A good bit of the interaction with members is initiated in the interest of staff purposes, including purposes that conjoin with those of chairmen, although there may be mutual staff–member benefit. In some agencies, means have been established for processing requests of individual

members for special staff assistance. They generally require the request to be handled by executive directors. The close ties between
these officials and chairmen may have a dampening effect on the
number of requests. Furthermore, the staff officials through whom
the requests are funneled have some control over staff responses. At
times biases exist against the use of staff resources by particular commissioners. One executive director commented that he would "think
twice" about authorizing a study to buttress a commissioner's position when it was contrary to that of the chairman.

Restraints may be imposed by chairmen. Some—not all by any
means—have actively discouraged close relationships between commissioners and staff. During most of his time, according to a former
Federal Power Commission member, "the staff was told not to talk
to commissioners." A former Federal Trade Commission member
commented, "You can't talk to the staff . . . . The chairman resents
it." A former staff official of that agency said, "I had strict orders
not to let commissioners direct the staff," and that any involvement
beyond the strict confines of case responsibilities was interpreted as
constituting efforts to "direct."

Stimulated by conditions and attitudes which associate chairmen
with staff in relationships which substantially exclude members, there
is a distinct tendency on the part of members who would like it otherwise to hold themselves aloof from staff. Some wish to avoid placing
the staff in a difficult position through, for example, asking for special
assistance in the development of a position differing from the chairman's. A former commissioner commented that when it came to taking
a position contrary to the "front office," "I would not want to put
the staff on the spot." Another reported an initial reluctance to interact with the staff and a feeling that it would be best "to stay away
from the staff in order to avoid putting them in a conflict situation."
Some members exercise restraint out of concern for the staff's work-
load, "so as not to overload the staff with idiosyncratic requests"
which would divert them from other responsibilities. For a commissioner to "make large demands on staff time" is seen as inappropriate.

Many members stand apart from work at the staff level because
of their sense of role and their personal interests. Action on matters
brought for formal resolution is viewed as the principal responsibility.
What has happened previously is of little moment. A former executive
director of one agency commented, "The commissioners were generally so tied up in cases that they did not concern themselves with
what the staff was doing." Other interpretations suggest a fundamental disinterest. One former chairman, in explaining the divorce of
commissioners from staff observed simply, "They did not bother to
inform themselves." A member of another agency reported an absence

of constraints on the access of commissioners to the staff, but, he added, "most members don't place demands on the staff. There is a lack of interest." Efforts to involve members systematically with staff outside the case routine lend support to these characterizations. Experiments in stimulating greater interaction related to general policy problems and to priorities, for example, often have floundered on the shoals of commissioner disinterest.

Although commissions and their individual members may find it difficult to manage staff work, they may and do influence staff work through their formal actions. Commissions with strong feelings on policy questions may provide collective leadership beyond the bounds of particular proceedings. Even when the collective body fails to guide the staff, one or a few assertive members may in part compensate and moderate the impact of chairmen on staff-level activities. There has been a fairly recent instance of this in the Federal Power Commission. And, reportedly, when Manuel Cohen and Byron Woodside were members of the Securities and Exchange Commission, "the staff knew the chairman's views might not prevail" because of their mastery of securities law with the result that staff inclinations toward the chairman's position were moderated by caution. However, the conditions which lead to direct, comprehensive, and sustained challenges by colleagues to leadership of the staff by chairmen occur quite infrequently.

Working Relationships

The personal predispositions of chairmen shape the nature and extent of directive activity and the means employed. There are several points about chairmen which are especially relevant in their relationships with staff. These include their own regulatory agendas, their sense of chairman and member roles, their "natural" leadership style and views of leadership requirements created by organizational conditions, and their expectations regarding their period of service, or the extent to which they see themselves as "passing through" with a brief period of time in which to make a mark on a few areas of special importance. Even when the driving forces are toward moderation in involvement with staff, chairmen remain of central significance for staff efforts. Staff will seek cues in the chairman's statements, comments, votes, and other acts as a means of informing themselves about his state of mind. A considerable amount of overt staff direction is unavoidable. "The chairman's job requires him to be an activist in relation to the staff," according to one in that position.

Chairmen generally work through a relatively small number of top staff members, typically including the heads of bureaus and offices. The chairman and these officials may be viewed as a leadership group, with the latter often standing in a cabinet-like relationship to the former. A chairman's most immediate impact is on these top officials; his influence on the rest of the staff usually runs through them. Thus the phrase, "the chairman's men," does not refer just to conditions of appointment and symbolic ties; it has operational meaning as well. A part of this meaning was suggested by Federal Communications Commission chairman Richard Wiley in congressional hearings in 1974 when he characterized himself and his top staff as comprising an "executive team." Among other activities, the "team" met at least once a week "to plan Commission agendas, to set priorities, and, most significantly, . . . to establish deadlines for everything the Commission does."[16]

Assistants to chairmen are key members of the leadership group, important in providing substantive direction to staff as they are in administrative matters. Assistants serve as alter egos, intimate advisors, often as surrogates, and not infrequently as deputy chairmen. They generally have detailed familiarity with the work of the agency and its personnel, provide information to the chairman regarding matters at the staff level, and communicate the chairman's concerns and views to the staff. They are, in a real sense, extensions of his eyes, ears, and hands, "in touch" with the staff, as one put it. And down "in the bowels" or "in the pits" of the agency, their word may be of considerable substantive consequence. One of the most common uses of assistants is in expediting decision processes through exerting pressure on staff to move quickly or assisting in resolution of conflict at the staff level. The substance of matters may be affected by their interventions. A former assistant who was quite active at the staff level characterized a significant portion of his efforts as "shirt sleeve" in nature. In addition to expediting matters, he was deeply involved in choices "on the broad outlines of staff effort" and in determining "the general lines of strategy" to be followed in important initiatives underway at the time. On occasion assistants have acted so vigorously and assertively that they have been viewed as "brow-beating" bureau heads. One former assistant commented that, "Although I never told bureau chiefs what to do, no one would ever believe it."

Working relationships between chairmen and staff take varied form. Some chairmen employ staff meetings extensively. One of the most enthusiastic in this connection was Joseph Swidler when chairman of the Federal Power Commission. As described by one of the regulars, there was a staff meeting each morning. The heads of bureaus and offices were generally there, and other staff members were often present. "Almost anything was discussed. It was very informal." The meetings were volatile at times. They were used in part to expedite the flow of work and to push deadlines. In the discussions, "the chairman spoke freely and bluntly." When things were not to his satisfaction, he would give "reprimands." What came from him was "not so much cues as directions" over a wide range of matters before the agency.

In another agency a chairman held weekly staff meetings with top officials. As he described it, the major focus of discussions was on the matters to be "aimed at" in the weekly commission meetings. He also used the sessions to understand the staff and their major undertakings and "to expose ideas with which the chairman may be concerned."

Considerable interaction between chairmen and staff officials may take place through means other than formal staff sessions. As one chairman put it, he was in "daily contact" with members of the staff. An Interstate Commerce Commission member reported an impression of frequent contact between the chairman and the top staff, and that "a lot of things happen that way."

Inevitably many of the working relationships between chairmen and staffs are such that other commissioners are not involved or even aware of them. They are not always excluded, however. Chairmen may bring and have brought commissioners and staff together on substantive matters outside the regular meeting agenda. When chairmen have held staff meetings, other commissioners have been invited to participate at times. But because of disinterest or a sense of the prerogatives of the chair, colleagues are rarely involved when chairmen concern themselves with matters at the staff level, even when opportunities are extended to them.

From time to time, a chairman appears who personally becomes deeply involved in the detailed supervision of staff work. Supervision may focus on administrative problems such as the expedition of case handling, or it may be extended to include substance. Two tendencies associated with chairmen who are deeply involved in the particulars of regulation are by-passing intermediate levels and dealing directly with lower echelon staff and handling affairs in the chairman's office which normally are the concern of staff. One chairman, for example, was characterized as having a pervasive impact on work at the staff level "through a variety of carefully orchestrated actions and direct and indirect contact with staff," despite a surface informality and guilelessness which masked a most expansive concept of position. Little escaped his attention, including opportunities to shape policy in accord with his own views. In this connection, he would on occasion draft language for rules he wished to have proposed, then send the material to the staff for refinement and processing.

The involvement of this chairman in the particulars of regulation exceeded that desired or attained by most others serving during the

1960s and 1970s. But, on occasion, placing immediate responsibility for specifics, such as drafting rules, in the chairman's office has been apparent. A desire to control for the sake of control may be involved. Considerations, such as slowness of regular processes when speed seems required, avoidance of premature publicity, and differences of opinion between the chairman's office and the staff, may also give impetus to the use of extraordinary approaches. As a case in point, the enlargement of the office of chairman of the Federal Communications Commission in recent years and the undertaking there of much that is generally considered to be staff work by the chairman's own staff or consultants may be attributed to such considerations.

The tendency of some chairmen to be concerned personally with the activities of lower-level staff may not be especially significant in the total scheme of things, but it does illustrate the rather extensive flexibility that exists regarding working relationships and the imprint that the style of a chairman may have. A brief look at a series of chairmen in two agencies will indicate the stylistic variations that may be observed even among highly influential chairmen. In the first agency, Chairman A was described as keeping close tabs on the work of the staff. He held frequent staff meetings. He was also quick to go immediately to the source of problems as he saw them. For example, when a letter drafted by a GS-7 staff member crossed his desk for signature and displeased him, his reaction would be vigorous and forthright. "Who wrote that letter? Peterson? Get that damned Peterson up here right now." And Peterson would quickly appear to receive the appropriate chastisement and direction.

In contrast, Chairman B, his successor, remained quite aloof from the staff. Direct relations with even top staff members were limited and irregular. He was away on speaking and other engagements quite a bit. In general, there was disinterest in the specifics of work at the staff level. Major reliance was placed on a few close staff associates to represent the chairman's general interests.

In the second agency, Chairman C, by all accounts, was in full and systematic command. He saw himself as the executive head of the agency. Throughout his tenure, there were regular staff meetings in which the subjects were minor as well as major issues. During the first part of his chairmanship, he was in frequent and direct contact with intermediate and lower-level staff members. Later, he began to rely more and more on his assistant to represent his interests at these points. Unquestionably, however, the influence of the office of the chairman remained impressive and pervasive.

His successor was more restrained in relationships with the staff because he was less experienced in the particular regulatory area, sensitive to the abrasions which remained from the aggressiveness of the previous regime, and more inclined toward intimate contact with his colleagues and decision-making at the commission level. Chairman D worked with top staff on an ad hoc basis and relied on the executive director to monitor staff activities. He had no personal assistant who represented him at the staff level.

The third chairman in this chain was more like the first than the second. Chairman E took a broad view of the prerogatives of the chair in the management of agency affairs. He was involved with staff members day by day, circumventing intermediaries. In administration, his involvement extended to such matters as approval of travel requests. In substantive matters, he made specific work assignments to lower-level staff, then monitored progress and reviewed the products. "When the staff made mistakes, they heard about it from the chairman."

These illustrations underscore a particularly important point regarding links between chairmen and staff: a principal factor determining the nature of lineages is the chairman himself, just as he is a principal factor in determining the association of colleagues with the staff outside formal commission gatherings.

The Impact of Chairmen on Staff Activity in Perspective

The characteristic roles of chairmen and their colleagues in regard to substantive work at the staff level appear to have developed in the same direction as roles in the areas discussed in previous chapters. Chairmen have more extensive access to staff. Access opportunities are joined with a basic receptivity on the part of staff to the exercise of leadership from the chair. The substantial capacity for influencing staff activity indicates that commission-level functions pertaining to staff direction have been integrated in the chairmanship to a greater extent than surface appearances suggest.

The claim of a former assistant in one agency that "We managed the staff from the chairman's office" is suggestive but probably exaggerated. Though the influence of chairmen may be substantial, there are boundaries. It is difficult, however, to mark them precisely and to define the influence of chairmen on regulatory processes and decisions which come through this connection with staff, although a general depiction may be offered with some confidence.

The influence of chairmen is easier to see and probably greater and more direct over the nature and form of staff activity or the regulatory agenda, priorities, and style reflected there than in the particulars of staff decisions or recommendations. Influence in particular matters may be substantial, however. There are limits, even concerning agenda, priorities, and style. These include efforts underway as a result of the initiatives of predecessors; external pressures such as from Congress; regulatory routines which must be performed; ingrained organizational perspectives and habits which, according to one chairman, can only be influenced "so much"; and the orientations and special interests of colleagues. Within the boundaries, a broad range of regulatory activity remains open to the influence of chairmen. The opportunities are sufficient to allow a chairman not particularly concerned with directing the staff to concede that he, of necessity, did so "in a general way."

If chairmen are "dominant" in regard to staff activity, as one characterized his position, what, more precisely, may they dominate or, if not dominate, substantially influence? They may influence the nature of discretionary activity and processes of conceptual formulation and reformulation in the critical choices made at the staff level. There are a variety of specific ways in which this occurs. Chairmen may initiate inquiries and studies and they may play a large role in the initiation of more formal staff efforts, such as rule-making proceedings and investigations. They may, under certain circumstances, stop staff efforts or block the results from reaching the commission for action. An assistant to a Federal Communications Commission chairman suggested the underlying dynamics when he observed, "In general, the staff would not make a major move without determining that at least we had no position." A former chairman of another agency, and one who indicated that he did not fully utilize the potential of the position in this regard, observed, "A strong chairman in a very real way can control what comes to the commission . . . . If he sees something coming he did not like, he could kill it." Another associated with that agency agreed, but added, "If you do it, you had better not let the others find out about it." He, incidentally, was one reputed to have exercised that type of influence. Chairmen may also influence the scope of staff-level activity as a recent Civil Aeronautics Board chairman reportedly did in an investigation of the political contributions of airline companies.[17] They may influence the pace of staff-level activity, causing speed or delay.[18] And they may influence the regulatory style reflected in staff activity, as did Paul Rand Dixon when chairman of the Federal Trade Commission. Early in his chairmanship, he made a number of speeches emphasizing the desirability of cooperative relations between the agency and the business community and education and voluntary compliance as means for eliciting correct business practices. "The staff got the message," and formal complaints decreased perceptibly.

The nature and form of regulatory activity bear a close relationship to the substantive results of that activity. Initiating, stopping, and influencing the scope or pace of action generally are intended to attain some substantive objective. Substantive impact may be more pointed. A former commissioner said, "Whether the issue is compliance or to close an investigation, the staff influence [on the commissioners] is almost always decisive. And the staff is subservient to the chairman. Their loyalty is to him." A person involved in another agency generalized that "Chairmen don't get shot down by the staff." Others tended to play down somewhat the influence of chairmen on the content of staff-prepared materials, reporting only a tendency for them to "slant to a slight degree toward the chairman's predilections."

Whatever the nuances and gradations of influence in particular situations, it is clear that in discretionary and non-adjudicatory matters, the chairman's views generally are given more weight by the staff than the views of other members, especially on matters that clearly are of importance to him. Under certain circumstances, chairmen may act purposefully to ensure that their views are known below and taken into account. They may have been directly involved with staff in preliminary stages. In other circumstances, including adjudicatory proceedings, it may be the staff's perception of the chairman's position, based upon a variety of cues, that is the key factor. Thus chairmen, without necessarily intending it, though many do, may have a substantial impact on work at the staff level, including what comes to the commissions to serve as a basis for decision. At times, depending on the meshing of circumstances and personality, the impact may be quite profound.

A particularly astute former chairman underscored the significance of relations with the staff in assessing the relative influence of chairmen and their colleagues in regulatory decisions: "The chairman's opportunity really is in terms of giving some direction to working papers before they get on the commission's agenda." The "working papers" which draw the attention of chairmen and concerning which some staff response to that attention may be expected are likely to be the important ones, those that involve critical rather than routine questions. But there is more to regulatory decision-making than staff work. The relative influence of chairmen and their colleagues when matters reach commissions for decision now becomes the focus of attention.

7.

Commission Decisions

John Robson became chairman of the Civil Aeronautics Board in 1975. The first major proceeding in which he participated concerned air fares. In that decision several important changes were made in how rates would be determined. The relationship between the arrival of Robson and the reflection of new approaches in rate-making is unclear. It is interesting, however, that one member and Robson's predecessor as chairman, Robert D. Timm, while agreeing with the decision in overall terms "objected to what he called precipitous and ad hoc changes in the board's rate-making philosophy."[1] Is it plausible that a change in the chairmanship might alter regulatory policy in a fundamental way? Such questions provide the focus for this chapter and constitute the final line of exploration into patterns of agency governance.

There are two modes of critical decisions at issue. The first consists of decisions of a substantive character which do not involve formal proceedings and which chairmen may make in behalf of their colleagues. They may be made, for example, in relations with Congress, other government agencies, and the regulated. The important questions regarding them, from the perspective of agency governance, concern the boundaries of the discretion which chairmen enjoy. The second mode includes decisions made collectively by the members. The important questions about them concern the relative impact of chairmen and their colleagues. Do chairmen have strategic resources to employ in decision-making, as they do in administrative and management areas, which are unavailable to their colleagues? Are there tendencies on the part of members to respond to the leadership of chairmen and to "go along" with them?

A General Characterization

In the summer of 1974, in the midst of deliberations on an important matter, a senior commissioner turned to a chairman and asked simply and bluntly, "What do you want?" Such directness in the relationship between chairmen and their colleagues may be uncommon. The incident does suggest, however, the central importance of chairmen in substantive decisions at the commission level. In general, data from interviews and other sources indicate that in substantive decision-making, the influence of chairmen in comparison with that of their colleagues is substantial, sometimes determinative. Chairmen typically can act for commissions in many areas beyond formal proceedings. In formal proceedings and other instances when there are collective decisions, the chairman's position has great impact.

A survey of dissent patterns in collective decisions provides substantiation for the latter part of the generalization. Reported decisions since 1961, to the extent they are available, indicate that chairmen dissent with much less frequency than their colleagues.[2] With only a few exceptions, the number of times chairmen dissent during their tenure can be counted on the fingers of one hand. Alan Boyd, the only Civil Aeronautics Board chairman whose tenure is completely covered by available documentation, dissented four times in full and twice in part during four years as chairman, from 1961 to 1965. During seven years as chairman of the Federal Maritime Commission, from 1962 to 1969, John Harllee dissented four times and did not participate on an equal number of occasions. His successor, Helen Delich Bentley, was not recorded in a dissenting role up into 1972. During more than eight years as chairman of the Federal Trade Commission, from 1961 to 1969, Paul Rand Dixon dissented twice. He was recorded as not participating once, as not concurring in the result once, and as preferring a different remedy once. Similarly, from 1961 to 1965, Joseph Swidler lodged two dissents to Federal Power Commission decisions. And, from 1961 to 1966, William Cary dissented once in full and once in part while chairman of the Securities and Exchange Commission. The large volume of formal decisions made an examination of the Federal Communications Commission difficult. However, a study of voting in the agency from 1963 through 1967 indicated that E. William Henry, whose chairmanship was during this period, dissented less often than any other member.[3] A recent analysis by a public interest group showed members voting with the chairman of the Federal Communications Commission, Richard Wiley, 97.6 percent of the time.[4]

On the record, then, chairmen are infrequently in the minority. Reported votes do not always reflect true positions, to be sure.

Compromise, including compromise by chairmen, is part of agency decision-making. Chairmen may feel it important to be recorded in the majority, and thus vote contrary to their convictions from time to time because of a belief in the importance of an appearance of unity and not to appear to have lost control. Even when the figures regarding dissents are discounted, a very substantial association of chairmen with majorities remains, giving support to the perceptions of participants.[5]

Although the leadership role of chairmen in substantive activities at the commission level is clear, generalizations about it must be taken with some caution. There is a lesser degree of agreement among the perceptions reported by participants than in other areas which have been explored. For example, the chairman of one agency asserted that in collective decisions, the chairman essentially has one vote. His influence depends upon the amount of initiative which is exerted, but that holds true for other members as well. In contrast, a former commissioner of that same agency commented, "I am unaware of any time in nine years when, if a chairman wanted, he could not carry the commission along with him." Differences may be taken as indications of the subtleties of the problem as well as uncertainties even among participants in regard to the forces at work.

As in previous chapters, the relative influence of chairmen and their colleagues is best understood in terms of the expectations which shape roles, resources of positions, interests of commissioners, and interests and concerns of chairmen. The context of decision-making at the commission level is an important conditioning factor. Complexity provides foundation and gives impetus to the emergence of a leadership role for chairmen.

Perspectives on Leadership

In chapter 1 it was suggested that a complex world surrounds much regulatory decision-making, marked by conflicting pressures, involvement with other institutions, and political, policy, and program vulnerability. It was also suggested that an important aspect of agency governance was the management of this complexity. Chairmen are in a unique position to assist colleagues in coping with the complex circumstances which they face.

The flavor of this complex world as it may condition relations between chairmen and their colleagues was suggested by Ray Garrett, Jr., chairman of the Securities and Exchange Commission, in congressional testimony. He began by noting that in several meetings of the commission each week, agendas may include any of the approximately three-hundred types of proceedings which fall within the agency's jurisdiction.

> In the course of a typical week, the Commission will almost certainly be required to consider whether to suspend trading in the securities of a dozen or more corporations for a 10-day period; whether to grant authority to its staff to issue subpoenas to investigate apparent violations of law on the part of both individuals and corporate or other business entities; whether, based upon the results of completed investigations, to institute lawsuits or administrative proceedings or refer matters to the Attorney General for criminal prosecution; whether to accept offers of settlement in the pending proceedings and actions or to appeal adverse decisions in court actions we have lost; and whether to participate as amicus curiae in private actions brought to enforce duties imposed by the Federal securities laws.
>
> In addition to enforcement and related matters, the Commission in a typical week considers a wide variety of regulatory questions concerning, for example, the necessity for new or amended Commission rules prohibiting fraudulent activities or regulating the conduct of national securities exchanges, broker-dealers, investment companies or investment advisers. Or the Commission may have an occasion to review the adequacy of rules that the exchanges or the National Association of Securities Dealers have adopted pursuant to their statutory self-regulatory responsibilities.[6]

The implications for the individual commissioner were indicated by Whitney Gillilland, a former judge and long-time member of the Civil Aeronautics Board. He commented, almost plaintively, that as a judge he could master problems in a way not possible as a commissioner.

> I could work on them and study them until I had my head around them and then decide, not always wisely, I am sure, but then I at last had self-satisfaction. This I can't do at the Civil Aeronautics Board. What I do is a constant compromise between mastery, or an effort to master problems that come along, and time, and reliance on other people's judgment.[7]

Those other people include the staff, but also they include the chairman directly and through his relationship with the staff.[8]

Some of the barriers to problem mastery stem from the number, variety, and technical complexity of issues and the time limitations with which all decision-makers must contend. Others are associated with the segmented character of regulatory efforts, especially when viewed from the perspective of commissioners. Segmentation occurs because decisions are often part of a developing series of related responses to a problem; because particular decisions have often been preceded by negotiations with interested parties in which members have not been involved; and because some of the decisions in program sequences have not been made by commissions *en banc,* but by staff and chairmen. Segmentation is less a problem for chairmen than for members. Their position causes them to be involved comprehensively and thus provides an integrated view of related activity. Both the reality and colleague perception of a superior view are important elements in relationships.

The initial response of the Interstate Commerce Commission to the fuel emergency of 1973–74 suggests some aspects of complexity including the segmented but related form of important regulatory choices. It contained the following parts: (1) a rule-making proceeding was instituted to ascertain changes in statutes required by the emergency; (2) special orders were issued regarding the recapture of increased costs by carriers; (3) rules were altered regarding "gateway" points in motor carrier certificates; (4) a policy statement was issued advising carriers on various points raised by the situation; (5) a special order was promulgated facilitating pooling of freight; (6) a series of informal meetings was called between the chairman and representatives of industry, labor, and carriers to explore problems and steps which might be taken by the commission; and (7) liaison was maintained with various federal agencies through the chairman and staff.[9]

Another example emphasizes the informal processes featuring chairmen and staff which anticipate formal action and concerns the Civil Aeronautics Board and minimum fare guidelines for trans-Atlantic charter flights in the 1974–75 period. According to trade reports, the stimulus for action was concern for the financial health of Pan American World Airways, and this was the fundamental problem at issue, not the level of fares per se. Commission approval of guidelines came after two years of discussion within the executive branch conducted under the aegis of Peter Flanigan of the White House staff. Participants included representatives of the Departments of State and Transportation and the Civil Aeronautics Board, specifically Robert Timm, the chairman. There were also separate discussions between Timm and the Secretary of Transportation. The controversy continued after the board's initial decision which was attacked by the Department of Justice, various consumer groups, charter lines, and tour operators. A suit filed by Justice early in 1975 caused the board to alter its stance.[10] But the illustrative point is the extensive and delicate preparatory work touching upon a wide range of interests in which the board was not centrally involved except through its chairman.

As Judge Gillilland's comments and these illustrations show, the image of regulatory decision-making as taking place under much the same conditions as judicial decision-making is a distortion. Especially in important matters, more is involved than simply the record and the specific issues it presents for resolution. And much of that which is additionally involved may be beyond the control and imperfectly in the ken of decision-makers with the exception, perhaps, of the chairman. The comprehensive involvement of chairmen not only allows them an opportunity to influence matters prior to commission consideration, it forces colleagues to rely on them for interpretations of and judgments about the critical points in decisions.

The characteristics of agency decision-making processes condition expectations regarding substantive leadership by chairmen. Most members and chairmen would probably agree that necessity and presidential designation provide the latter with a basic charter as "the leader and pacesetter," with special responsibility "to get things done," as one commissioner put it. A special responsibility to at least offer substantive direction to colleagues is implied. But when the problem becomes determining the precise meaning of serving as leader and pacesetter and getting things done, the discretion to be allowed chairmen and their influence in collective choices, ambiguities and even contradictions begin to emerge.

The view of commissioners regarding the proper range of discretion to be allowed chairmen when collective decision-making is not required are hardly systematic and comprehensive in character, but there is a tendency to define the prerogatives of chairmen rather permissively. Guiding the work of the staff in behalf of the commission is one pertinent area. Another concerns the external relationships of the agency, even when agency positions must be formulated. In the Federal Trade Commission, for example, according to an informed observer, external relationships "are considered by the others to be the prerogative of the chair." However, a former member noted, after expressing essential agreement, the prerogative is qualified by the expectation that others be "advised on important things." Allowing chairmen considerable latitude in external relationships extends to congressional matters in most instances. Members of the Federal Communications Commission and the Interstate Commerce Commission appear to view the prerogatives of the chairman in this respect in somewhat narrower terms. Their chairmen have had occasional difficulties, although a sense is present that the responsibilities of chairmen are different from those of members and that there are certain decision-making perquisites which attach to the position.

In the abstract, commissioners may be generous in their views regarding the discretion of chairmen in substantive matters in other than formal proceedings, but the boundaries do not necessarily remain fixed. They are subject to adjustment based upon circumstances, especially the degree to which the chairman is trusted. The greater the degree of trust, the greater the latitude that is allowed. As trust diminishes, the more closely the others will attempt to monitor the chairman and to become involved in matters which otherwise they would leave alone. The phenomenon of trust will be examined in a later portion of this chapter.

When there must be collective decisions, there is fairly general agreement among members that it is appropriate for chairmen to assert views about the nature of problems and desirable course of action from the perspective of their position as chairman. There also is general agreement that it is appropriate for chairmen to make determinations regarding the processes to be used for reaching a commission decision. Thus a measure of control is sanctioned regarding agenda content and working procedures at the commission level.

Commissioners are in less agreement about the weight that should be accorded the chairman's position in arriving at a decision. For some, the chairman's position on any matter is seen as carrying no special weight because it is that of the chairman. It may be proper for a chairman to attempt to lead, but it is not right for members to set aside their critical faculties and simply follow. An Interstate Commerce Commission member captured this perspective. After reporting that the chairman's vote did not seem to count more than any other, he commented, "The chairman is expected to supply leadership. Even if you are opposed, it gives you something to shoot at."

Other members distinguish between adjudicatory and non-adjudicatory matters, such as rule-making or legislative positions. "In the judicial role, commissioners are like judges, free to dissent," one asserted. In other matters, unanimity becomes a matter of institutional interest, if not necessity, apparently the traditional orientation in that agency. For this member, it is proper to cast aside doubt in non-adjudicatory determinations and support the position of the chairman in behalf of institutional well-being.

Some members do believe, however, that there are adjudicatory circumstances in which it is appropriate to follow the chairman's leadership and present a united front because of the controversial character of the issue and the likelihood that criticism will focus on the chairman. A former commissioner said, "The chairman has to take the flack. So unless you feel very strongly, in effect you say to the chairman, 'You make the decision.'" A former member of another agency put it in very similar form. The chairman is the recipient of the "brickbats." Members "want to help," so they go along if the chairman's position is not strikingly different and support of it does not mean "the total surrender of principles."

In summary, although it is evident that expectations of members regarding the places of chairmen and commissioners in substantive determinations do not all move in the same direction, a special role for chairmen in non-adjudicatory matters has strong foundation. Differences are more apparent in regard to adjudication, but even here some basis for attaching special weight to the chairman's views are to be found.

Chairmen generally, if not universally, take a broad view of appropriate independent action and see substantive leadership and positive efforts to influence their colleagues as called for by their position. Notions regarding the exercise of influence in collective decisions in other than formal proceedings are especially generous, but not much more so than those of colleagues. Differences among chairmen are more apparent in regard to their role in formal proceedings, and especially in adjudicatory matters. They split into two groups on the appropriateness of purposeful efforts to influence those decisions. Some chairmen emphasize collegiality. One, in explaining his philosophy of restraint, commented that everyone "was supposed to be on the same team." On the same point, another emphasized that "we [he and his colleagues] all got here the same way," through presidential appointment and Senate confirmation. Accordingly, as far as possible, chairmen should place themselves on the same footing with other members when decisions are made. Although the resources of position may still come into play, the impact of chairmen is moderated. Chairmen of this persuasion are not necessarily reluctant to assert judgments or to refrain completely from attempting to influence their colleagues. Instead, the resources emphasized tend to be personal rather than positional and to be those that, theoretically, are available to all, such as expertise and the logic of argument.

Other chairmen take a much larger, even aggressive, view of their obligations to collective decision-making. They see leadership to be a central responsibility. As one put it, "Part of the chairman's job is to get three votes for what he wants done." Chairmen of this type do not attempt to influence each decision or to use the advantages of position in unrestrained fashion. But they are distinguished from those in the first group by the idea that chairmen properly seek to influence their colleagues in important substantive determinations as chairmen and not as just another member, by the idea that special weight across the board should be attached to their views, and by the prospect that the resources of position will be employed purposefully to influence decisions.

Only a few chairmen serving during the period under examination fit comfortably into the first group. Most belong in the second. Even among them, variations in behavior appear; some have broader interests and are more vigorous than others. For now, however, the salient point is that chairmen often have notions of substantive leadership in collective choice that differ from those of some colleagues. Divergent notions on such a fundamental matter are a limit of sorts on chairmen and their influence, and are at least a potential source of tension in agency decision-making processes.

The Resources of Position

There are similarities between the resources associated with the position of chairman in substantive decision-making and in agency management. For the most part, the relevant resources stem from the general management prerogatives of chairmen, and especially those which affect substantive work of the staff, their visibility and responsibilities in relation to the world outside the agency, and the conventional functions of the chairman or presiding officer. The resources of position may enhance the influence of chairmen in natural ways, but they also may be employed purposefully. The relevant resources fall into three basic categories. As in the administrative area, there are knowledge and process resources. To these may be added as a separate category staff output resources.

Staff output resources concern the impact of the chairman on the substantive work of the staff. It has been seen that chairmen may have an impact on the staff work that serves as a basis for commission action. Staff recommendations are quite influential in commission decision-making. Thus the influence of chairmen on staff recommendations is translated into influence above. The close ties between chairmen and the staff are also means and support for independent initiatives of substantive import. They contribute to the discretion of chairmen concerning matters not requiring commission decisions.

Knowledge resources provide chairmen with access to information and expertise beyond that available to other members. Their relatively greater involvement with staff and the outside world are key. Chairmen are in a position to know more than their colleagues about staff initiatives underway, the content of materials to be presented as a basis for action, and the circumstances surrounding those materials. They are in a position to know more about the aims and purposes of those outside who are interested in the agency's work and, in general, about the political dimensions of the agency's environment. A former member of the Civil Aeronautics Board observed, "Members can get locked behind their doors." A picture of commissioners in monkish cells pouring over legal parchments is amusing to contemplate but it, of course, would hardly be accurate. A characterization of them as "not quite in the mainstream," offered by a former Federal Power Commission member, is probably apt. Chairmen may have, as they do in the Federal Maritime Commission, "at their disposal all the facts at the disposal of the agency," including facts not found in the record. Chairmen are the focal point for contact between the agency and its environment. According to a Federal Power Commission member, it is the chairman to whom interested outsiders talk. They "just don't come around" to the others. A close observer of the Interstate Commerce Commission commented that prior to the 1969 reorganization, when industry spokesmen came to call, they generally called on all eleven members. Since 1969 their visits increasingly have stopped with the chairman![11]

What is made of the access that chairmen have to information and expertise depends upon the individual. Perhaps the most important consequence of knowledge resources for the influence of chairmen is that members often perceive chairmen, because they are in that position, as "possessing a lot of information others do not have," according to one. Another said, "The chairman is presumed to know more." The perception of differences adds to the weight of a chairman's views and the members' responsiveness to his leadership, including acceptance of his actions outside the bounds of formal proceedings. Also, members must rely on the chairman for assistance in contending with regulatory complexities and for interpretations and integration of factors impinging on their decisions. Simply put, on many matters they must take the chairman's word.

Process resources allow chairmen to affect, if not control, how commissions make decisions which, in turn, may have an impact on the ultimate choices themselves. The means concern the general environment in which decisions are made, the decision-making agenda, and the setting and course of commission deliberations.

The larger decision-making environment includes the broad pressures which impinge on an agency from those interested in and affected by its work, and the degree of calm or turmoil and stability or flux which surrounds it. Impinging social, economic, and political forces are more significant determinants than the actions of any one man, obviously. However, as spokesman and, in a sense, agency representative to the world outside, and as one held by outsiders to be quite influential, a chairman may affect environmental conditions.[12]

Perhaps the best known example is Chairman Newton Minow's characterization of television programing as a "vast wasteland." His critique was a personal one and had not been discussed formally with the other Federal Communications Commission members. As his colleagues listened to the speech in which it was put forward, they were "horrified," according to one of them. Although the tangible results measured by commission action and industry behavior can be questioned, the climate with which the agency functioned and the problem agenda which it faced in subsequent years were affected in substantial ways along the lines intended by Minow.

As in this example, many times when chairmen speak they are reflecting a personal rather than an agency point of view. The distinction is easily lost, and a personal expression may be taken as an authoritative agency position. Whether views expressed are seen as personal or not, they may lead to changes in expectations of agency publics and staffs and ultimately to policy changes. They may, in fact, define situations and spark reactions in such a way as to make a particular course of action all but inevitable.[13]

One former chairman, who saw the capacity to speak and to be listened to as a major instrument of leadership, indicated some specific uses. Statements can "flush out problems." They can be employed to indicate to the regulated the issues the commission is thinking about which, in turn, focuses attention on and contributes to the definition of particular problems. Statements may stimulate some initiatives on the part of the regulated in which they "come back" to the agency with relevant proposals. The policy implications of commission decisions may be clarified by statements when decisions themselves cause confusion, thus allowing a chairman to articulate agency intentions according to his perceptions.

This chairman was referring to public statements and speeches. Similar purposes can be served in informal interactions. Chairmen at times have substantive discussions with interested parties—with industry leaders, for example—which commissioners do not attend. In such circumstances, chairmen have considerable freedom of expression and opportunities for impact.

Members have become irritated with chairmen regarding their public statements and their sessions with outsiders.[14] But, in general, chairmen seem to enjoy considerable freedom. When they purport to speak for their colleagues and submit their remarks for review, that review ordinarily is not exacting. Sherman J. Maisel's conclusions, based upon his experience as a member of the Federal Reserve Board, are broadly applicable. In matters such as congressional testimony, given the initiating and drafting responsibilities of chairmen, their "personal judgments can, and frequently do, dominate a statement." Although alterations may come as a result of review by colleagues, "most final statements follow closely the Chairman's original draft."[15] In an agency in which commissioners are somewhat sensitive about collective prerogatives, a staff member described the review process as being essentially *pro forma* and required changes as minimal and inconsequential. A member of another agency where such sensitivities have been apparent also reported that members generally accept the chairman's sense of the commission's position for transmission to the outside world.[16]

Another process resource of chairmen, and one of the most important, concerns regulatory action, of which there are two related parts. One concerns the initiative of agency actions of substantive consequence and the ability of chairmen to act independently in important matters. The other concerns control over the particulars of commission meetings and the implications of that control for influencing collective decisions.

Chairmen have substantial discretion in regard to both. They must judge whether collective attention is necessary in many instances. If it is called for, the chairman determines the form of that attention and whether the commission will decide, discuss the matter, or simply be informed after a decision has been made elsewhere or action taken.[17] Initiatives of considerable substantive importance may be undertaken by chairmen, with staff, and without prior commission approval. The control exercised over commission action may allow chairmen to exclude their colleagues and reserve agency authority to themselves. Although the extent and circumstances of such independence are difficult to specify, indications are that it is not uncommon and that the problems dealt with in this manner often are delicate, better handled informally, and perhaps not clearly subject to the authority of the agency. Election of an informal over a formal approach to a problem is illustrated by adjustments in air fares in the mid-1960s. The chairman of the Civil Aeronautics Board, convinced that fare reductions were in order, indicated to airline officials that institution of special discount fares, such as for students, might be a way to avoid a formal board investigation. The recent introduction of the "children's hour" on network television is an illustration of action beyond agency authority. Richard Wiley, chairman of the Federal Communications Commission, brought the concept of restricting the early prime-time period to family oriented programing forcefully to the attention of the networks; he proposed the idea to them in "a few friendly chats." The networks agreed to the concept and implemented it. The commission could not have ordered the action, nor did the networks have to make the programing adjustment. Sponsorship of the concept by the chairman of the Federal Communications Commission seemed to be the critical factor.[18]

There will be further discussion of chairmen as independent decision-makers a bit later in connection with another process resource, freedom of movement. But a measure of control over initiatives is fundamental, allowing chairmen to elect to pursue significant regulatory strategies independently of their colleagues and collective determinations. They may, at their own discretion, employ agency resources, including the prospect of formal proceedings distasteful to the regulated, to achieve regulatory results. The extent to which they act independently in placing matters on the action agenda in preference to involving their colleagues is to a considerable extent up to them, especially in the gray areas in which agency influence rather than authority is being employed.

Another aspect of the influence of chairmen over initiatives stems from a tendency of colleagues to await their expressions in considering significant departures from established regulatory approaches or responses to emergent problems, even when collective responsibility is clearly present. In the Civil Aeronautics Board, for example, members expect the chairman "to open the conversation." Although members may indicate concern and put forth ideas, the chairman's interest is critical for serious and sustained consideration. Without that interest, there will not be focused attention. Thus, there is a veto capacity in the chair regarding deliberations beyond the formal case docket, especially those involving the conceptual underpinnings of regulation. But also, the expectation that chairmen will open the conversation allows them to have the first say. "Getting first crack" at a problem, in the words of one chairman, may have a substantial impact on the position that ultimately emerges.

Chairmen generally are responsible for organizing the particular agendas which govern commission meetings. They may shape the agendas to enhance their influence, although most of the items which appear are routine and without strategic or tactical interest for anyone. Delaying consideration of an item in the face of a possible adverse outcome is probably the most common use of the opportunity. There also may be acceleration. A former chairman gave an illustration. In an important and sensitive policy issue, after initial discussion with his staff regarding the positions of his colleagues, he "sized 'em up." Finding that he needed one more vote, he promptly "got him." He moved quickly thereafter to bring the matter before the commission, and the vote went as he had expected. In his opinion, "If there had been a delay, it would never have gotten out."[19]

In addition to agendas, there are a multitude of matters related to commission decision-making processes which are susceptible to some degree of control by chairmen. Individually, they may seem trivial. Collectively they constitute a substantial resource which may be employed, as Maisel put it, to "shape debate" and to give chairmen various other strategic and tactical advantages.[20] Responsibility for commission gatherings beyond regular meetings, presiding over meetings, and freedom of movement seem to be of special importance.

For the most part, chairmen determine when and for what purposes commissions will meet in addition to regular sessions. Special meetings occur on their grounds and on their terms. The uses of special meetings vary extensively. Purposes may range from general discussion of regulatory problems and priorities for the future, to reaching concrete agreements. A chairman's capacity to orchestrate meetings to suit his purposes is quite large and has been used with considerable effect, such as to force consideration of matters of importance to him and to forge positions on sensitive issues.[21]

The prerogatives of the chair are significant even in regular formal meetings, but they are qualified by protocols regarding the presence of staff, the order of voting, and other aspects of commission deliberations. In the Interstate Commerce Commission, for example, decisions are made in a setting which is nearly as private as that of the Supreme Court and through a process that is no less well established in tradition. Whereas Interstate Commerce Commission decisions are made in an environment which is sheltered even from the staff and where deliberations are quite formal in character, Securities and Exchange Commission traditions, no less well established, provide for relative openness of deliberations to staff and informality in discussions. The patterns are so well set in these agencies that they probably could not be altered even if a chairman wished. But in other settings, chairmen may change conditions to facilitate decision-making and to add to their influence. Alterations in regard to the presence of staff at meetings exemplify the capacity and its uses. Chairmen may see the presence of staff as an advantage, and one chairman was reported to have "surrounded the members with staff expertise." Purposes may also be seen as served by exclusion of staff. Whatever the choice, in some agencies chairmen have been able to alter arrangements according to their view of their interests.[22]

Agency norms may also limit the discretion of chairmen in presiding. But even small matters, such as the order in which members present their views and the timing of a chairman's own interventions, may affect deliberations in critical ways. Maisel's comments regarding the uses of the chair by Federal Reserve Board chairmen William Martin and Arthur Burns in the Open Market Committee suggest the impact that may be attained. They behaved somewhat similarly.

> If no critical questions threatened or if decisions seemed fairly cut and dried, they would act in a relaxed manner, allowing discussion to wander and calling the question only when everyone was completely talked out. On the other hand, when a matter was critical or when they were in doubt as to how the final decision would go, they did not hesitate to state their views early in the meeting and to interject them strongly as the debate developed. They used such a tactic only occasionally, but when they did the impact was consider-

able. A strong statement by the Chairman early in the meeting is influential
and transforms the debating atmosphere.[23]

As the presiding officer, a chairman can focus attention on items,
and thus impose a personal agenda on the formal one. A brief, hand-
written list was carried into meetings by one chairman, indicating
those decisions he wanted that day. Chairmen may also cut off or
extend debate as a means of affecting outcomes. Matters may be sent
back to the staff when it appears that members are moving toward an
unacceptable conclusion. Additional time and staff work may cause
directions to be altered.

Chairmen also have opportunities at the point decisions are made.
Maisel mentions the importance of being able "to put votes in a form
most likely to promote their own position."[24] They may also be
required to sum up, or to state what has been decided. For example,
after hearing oral argument, Federal Trade Commission members
ordinarily come to a tentative decision following a brief discussion.
That decision is conveyed orally to the opinion writer. In the Civil
Aeronautics Board, after the board decides what it wishes to do, an
opinion writer is called into the meeting and given oral instructions.
Those who guide these critical discussions and give instructions to
staff who draft the decisions, the chairmen in these instances, have a
final and perhaps influential say. No two agencies conduct their
affairs at the point of decision and opinion preparation in the same
way. Whereas the *modus operandi* of the Federal Trade Commission
and the Civil Aeronautics Board may provide advantages to chairmen,
the situation may be different in other agencies. In the Federal Power
Commission, for example, after the commission has reached a position, the chairman assigns responsibility for overseeing the preparation of a decision to one of the members. He does make the assignment, however. In the Securities and Exchange Commission, the
members debate the issues before the lawyers from the Office of
Opinions and Review who will draft the decision.[25]

A final resource related to the setting and course of commission
deliberations and attached to the position of chairman may be generally characterized as freedom of movement. Emmette S. Redford
has suggested that regulatory decision-making involves a "search for
concurrence" among a complex of interests.[26] In large matters the
search extends far beyond the commission's meeting room. When
this is the case, and it often is, chairmen are critical links in the
chains of communications and in processes of negotiation. The involvement into which they are thrust by their position requires chairmen to speak authoritatively for their agencies, as in negotiations
with congressional leaders about changes in securities laws,[27] in the
complex negotiations of Dean Burch resulting in compromises

reflected in Federal Communication Commission rules governing CATV systems,[28] or in the negotiations between the chairman of the Federal Maritime Commission and representatives of foreign governments. Once agreements are reached in negotiations, it is very difficult for colleagues to reject the understandings and take divergent positions. Freedom of movement in the outside world is an especially important resource because so much that is truly significant in policy terms involves negotiations with other interests.

There is an aspect of freedom of movement that may be significant in smaller matters, in addition to the larger. It may be designated as corridor freedom. In a recent analysis, it was reported that when there was disagreement among his major economic advisors, President Lyndon B. Johnson would send Joseph Califano to "flit among them, like a pollinating bee" to secure some resolution.[29] Corridor freedom refers to the capacity to move about within the agencies in a manner that affects decisions.

It is difficult to grasp much that is specific about the interactions among commission members outside meeting rooms. Prior to formal collective considerations and during considerations when matters are subject to elongated attention, there is informal interaction, however. Members and their staffs try to divine the perspectives and positions of others and perhaps influence them. Even after an initial determination, there may be efforts like that of one chairman who, when finding himself on the short end of a vote, "worked like hell to turn it around." On larger policy questions that are an issue over time, the leadership problem is to build and maintain a coalition that will hold under pressure.[30] But turning it around may also be at issue in such cases.[31] The interactions among decision-makers may assume a bargaining coloration. Chairmen and their staffs enjoy greater bargaining opportunities because of greater freedom of movement. Particularly when a commission is stalemated, chairmen are expected to supply leadership through informally negotiating the resolution of differences. The expectation supplies both opportunities and a basis for action, allowing a chairman, as one put it, to "get around" on sensitive matters.

In summary, there is a rather substantial array of resources which attach to the position of chairman and which may be employed in substantive decision-making at the commission level. Colleagues are not completely bereft in the areas that have been discussed, but there is a distinct disparity.

The Interests of Commissioners

In the discussion of decision-making concerning organizational resources, structure, and processes, it was suggested that when the interests of other commissioners are examined, some rather significant reasons for deferring to chairmen become apparent. When the interests of commissioners are examined in relation to substantive decision-making it again seems that those interests are served to a certain extent by recognizing and being responsive to the leadership of chairmen.

There are two basic points about the alignment of commissioners with chairmen in substantive decision-making which must be delineated at this point. First, interests, in combination with other factors, create an initial disposition on the part of some members to support a chairman in matters about which he feels strongly. It is true that chairmen from time to time find themselves in the position of Newton Minow who, according to a close associate, "never had four votes for anything." But the more common circumstance seems to be for chairmen to start with a core of votes, if not a majority. Even in the Federal Communications Commission, this may be the case more often than not. One informed observer concluded that, at least in the 1967 period, Rosel Hyde, as chairman, "could count on at least three of the seven commissioners to support just about any stand he chose to take in any given case."[32] Second, members in the minority facing a majority which includes the chairman may ultimately join the majority. The fact that the majority contains the chairman is critical, if not determinative, for their turn about.

Why are some members predisposed to align themselves with chairmen, and why do others join with chairmen on particular issues when, acting alone, they would take a different stance? A former commissioner who often resisted the lure of alignment observed, "All the pressures are in the direction of being a team man." The dissenter's role is not a comfortable one, even though it may bring a certain renown. Severe costs are associated with standing apart from the majority, especially on a consistent basis, even though in theory there may be perfect freedom to do so. The smallness and relative intimacy of the commissions as decision-making bodies, as well as a sense of institutional interests, generate strong incentives for being a team player. To be a team player generally involves accepting the chairman as captain of the team. The interests of members in harmonious working relationships with their colleagues and an absence of distressing conflict at the interpersonal level may be quite potent. Even for the strongest willed, it is not easy to suffer continually the hostility of a chairman who feels his leadership has been rejected. A desire to be liked is not to be discounted as a strong motive in the behavior of members. And to be liked by the chairman may be especially important.[33]

Some of the more tangible costs of being on the outs with a chairman were indicated in chapter 3. To recapitulate briefly, in a variety of ways chairmen, through the distribution of perquisites and courtesies, can affect the place of a member in the agency scheme. Items range from facilitating the operation of the member's personal office, to opportunities for travel and speeches,[34] to commodities of considerable significance in the substantive work of the agency. Information is a prime example of a commodity with which chairmen are generally well supplied and which may be shared. A former commissioner, after commenting on the differences in the flow of information moving in and out of the chairman's office and that of the other commissioners, described one chairman as generally keeping the others informed about what was happening. "He was good about that." He did not have to share to the extent he did, and the fact that he did go beyond what was minimally required was seen as a positive aspect of his chairmanship.

The impact of chairmen on the degree of participation of members in the substantive work of the agencies is less than in administrative and management matters, but there is some discretion. Chairmen may approach their responsibilities so as to include other members through consulting extensively. Even though outcomes may not be changed as a result of discretionary consultation, the act of consultation itself is highly valued by members. Not only may the sense of meaningful participation be heightened, but members are provided opportunities to press substantive interests in contexts that might be closed to them except for the chairman's willingness to open the door.[35]

For some members, a supportive disposition may be founded in part on the involvement of chairmen in their appointment or, prospectively, their reappointment. Chairmen often are concerned with these matters. A former chairman commented that one should demand, as he did, a hearing in appointment decisions as a condition of accepting the position. William Cary said that while with the Securities and Exchange Commission in the 1960s, he "took the position that the selection of my colleagues was something in which I would like to exert as much influence as possible."[36] Another former chairman of this period characterized the nature of his interests in such matters. When there was a vacancy to be filled and he was discussing the matter with John Macy, in charge of recruitment at the White House, he would say to Macy: "Get me a guy who is bright, committed to the public interest, diligent, and who will vote the right way—my way. And if you can't find someone with all of these, the last is the most important. I will take the last." The precise impact of chairmen is shrouded. Not all chairmen are inclined to become involved, or are seen as influential.[37] However, in the lore of various agencies, there is enough about the suspected critical involvement of chairmen in appointment decisions to give credence to the prospect.[38]

Alignment with the chairman may come because it is concluded that institutional well-being is best served by the presentation of a solid front in critical matters. Split decisions, some members fear, may be taken as signs of agency weakness and indecision. Division may also stimulate pressures aimed at particular members intended to change their position, and thus change outcomes. Exposing members to pressures of this type may be costly in the particular case, injurious to the members who are the target of pressure, and harmful to the institution. Another and related advantage of being aligned with the chairman is that justification of a position is eased. To be with the chairman is to benefit from his greater visibility and his capacity to defend what has been done. To stand apart is to be exposed, and not only required to defend the position taken on the merits, but also to justify voting against the chairman. At the least, the second condition complicates the first. The substantive objectives of members may also cause them to "go along" in most cases, but to press selectively on points of particular concern from time to time. Strategic sense may suggest that, "You don't press issues not worth pressing," as the attitude of members of one agency was described. A member of another agency indicated the orientation in describing the dilemma he faced as a new commissioner and its resolution. "I came to the philosophical position that I could be a chronic dissenter and not accomplish anything. Or I could meld my thoughts into the final decision process." He elected the latter course, hoping to influence the chairman and the majority in some respects as a result of a willingness to join them.

Interests which press in the direction of agreement and support for the position of the chairman must be kept in perspective. Members have their individual substantive orientations and objectives. They may bring or develop expertise in particular areas which places them in a leadership role with chairmen as followers. They may be committed to certain positions so strongly that they will not yield and will express disagreement with the majority. By and large, however, members are political men, and strong views are often tempered by political sensitivity. As characterized by one observer, members understand that there are bound to be differences, but they also understand that "they have been thrust together to do certain things. It is not in their interest to screw up their relationships." This suggests a certain toleration of differences but also a reluctance to carry disagreement to the point at which relationships are fouled, especially concerning chairmen. Such orientations buttress leadership by chairmen in important matters.

The Realization of Potential

In regulatory processes, then, there is a pronounced tendency for members to go along with the views of chairmen and to allow them extensive discretion.[39] This tendency is associated with the characteristics of the position itself, regardless of who the chairmen are. But the uses of the position and the extent to which the potential for leadership and independent action is realized may be affected substantially by the individuals holding the position.

When the question is put, "What are the qualities that seem related to effective leadership in a collegial setting?" the responses, understandably, suffer from imprecision. One former commissioner emphasized their "intangible" character, reducing the problem to a mood resulting from the interplay of a complex of factors hardly to be understood. Chairmen are only slightly more specific. To one, it is the ability to "command respect." For another, chairmen lead through "the force of personality and intellect." And for yet another, it is "the respect of your colleagues and their assumption that you know what the work is about." In expressing a similar perspective, a chairman reputed to be quite an effective leader said that if a chairman is well versed and has good relations with people he can provide direction. "These guys will acquiesce in and expect you to do things that they would not accept if they knew more about them."

The evidence suggests with a bit more specificity than these statements provide that there are a number of personal characteristics which bear on the extent to which the potential of the position will be tapped. They pertain to the interests of chairmen, their expertise, their political standing, and the nature of the working relationships they establish with their colleagues.

The interests of chairmen are of fundamental importance for the extent to which they will act independently and seek to influence their colleagues and for the particular directions in which they will push. A substantial number of chairmen serving during the 1960s and 1970s had wide-ranging interests and asserted their views across a broad spectrum of decision-making activity, using all the resources and opportunities at their command. The largest number, however, were somewhat selective, concentrating on a few policy fronts as a means for leaving their marks. Realization of the complexities of problems, limitations on agency resources, exhaustibility of political capital, and the possibility of a relatively brief tenure in office lead to a focus on a few major priorities. Consequently, a good bit of agency activity, especially the routine matters, continues without the special imprint of chairmen.

Expertise is a critical quality in the exercise of leadership. There are two senses in which it is important. One is the general expertise of the sort developed by years of involvement in matters relating to the work of the agency. Expertise of this type is of obvious utility, and it also appears associated with the standing of the chairman with the regulatory community and with his colleagues and staff. A chairman who cannot claim such expertise has barriers to his leadership to overcome. The other sense in which expertise is important relates to mastery of particular matters coming before the commission for decision. Mastery of the particulars, which can be developed through preparation, is an antidote for the lack of extensive background. Whether there is a strong background or not, the willingness of chairmen to employ their knowledge resources and to prepare on substantive matters is critical, as it is for any member of a commission. But a prepared chairman, given other advantages, is in a stronger position than a prepared member, especially in the struggle to attract members who are not fully briefed. Furthermore, chairmen, it could be argued, are in a better position to prepare in the strategic sense, or, as one put it, to already have "set the wheels in motion" through groundwork with staff and selected colleagues. A former chairman noted for his careful planning and preparation and who generally got his way in the face of ill-prepared adversaries commented, with just a hint of disgust in his voice, "Imagine. Going into a meeting with only a few brief notes from an assistant and expecting to get a result there."

For some, the political standing of chairmen, especially in the White House, adds to the "aura of power" which surrounds them and their ability to lead, in addition to having significance for appointment questions. The evidence upon which members base judgments regarding standing comes largely from assumptions, rumors, and deductions from the nature of past associations. As a case in point, the prior relationships between President Johnson and Charles Murphy, chairman of the Civil Aeronautics Board, and his successor, John Crooker, were of consequence in the internal workings of the agency. Occasionally, presidents may provide indications themselves. A commissioner appointed during the early 1960s had these comments from President John F. Kennedy: "I'm not trying to tell you how to vote. But we have a reform commission down there. When all things are equal, I would like you to go along with the chairman." When President Lyndon B. Johnson personally presided at the White House swearing-in of Manuel Cohen as chairman of the Securities and Exchange Commission with the other members and substantial numbers of the staff present, the meaning of the occasion was clear to the audience.

A loss of standing in the White House may diminish the influence of chairmen. One Kennedy appointee lacking connections with the

Johnson administration was quite certain that the transition reduced his capacity to lead. In the Federal Maritime Commission, where the chairman had been President Kennedy's superior in the U.S. Navy and had led a White House initiated reorganization, after the assassination it was "a new ball game."

Initially, expertise, including the evidence of it in the way a chairman executes his responsibilities, and political standing may be the most important things about chairmen which bear on the receptivity of colleagues to their leadership. Over time, style and personality, as reflected in working relationships, grow in importance. What, from the perspective of colleagues, are the attributes beyond expertise and political standing which serve to enhance their acceptance of and responsiveness to a chairman's leadership? When asked this question, the answer of one commissioner was, "Ability to make the collegial system work." And when asked what was necessary for that, the answer was, "I don't know." But some things can be said. It does not appear that a chairman's style in interpersonal relationships, viewed narrowly, is of great significance for leadership capacity. Commissioners generally are quite tolerant of personal idiosyncracies. Chairmen who tend to be aggressive, assertive, insistent on their positions, impatient in deliberations, and bombastic in dealing with their colleagues do not seem to be any more or less effective than those manifesting opposite stylistic characteristics.[40] Personal feelings of warmth or antagonism may be generated and become a factor in particular circumstances but, overall, it is not possible to explain much about the comparative leadership effectiveness of chairmen in these terms. Members tend to respond to and evaluate chairmen more on the basis of considerations such as competency and the results achieved than on personal likes and dislikes.[41]

There is one sense, however, in which style is clearly significant. It concerns how a chairman relates to colleagues in those matters they consider to be of major importance and which they perceive as involving joint responsibilities. At the beginning of his tenure, a chairman has a considerable amount of "acceptance capital,"[42] but a person who worked closely with one of the most potent chairmen serving in recent years noted, "The chairman just has one vote. And over time, if he doesn't make an effort to bring the other commissioners along, he ends up undercutting himself."

How may chairmen undercut themselves? Not through a low-place finish in a personality contest, whatever the criteria, or even periodic and pointed expressions of differences. They undercut themselves through negation of the concept of collegiality as it has come to be defined in practice. That definition contains within it a recognition that there are basic differences in the roles of chairmen and members in substantive affairs. It does not follow, in the view of members, that the commission as a whole should be pushed into insignificance or ignored, and that they should be marked with the stigmata of second-class citizenship. Chairmen undercut themselves, then, when their actions indicate disrespect for their colleagues and reveal an intent to reduce the role of others beyond acceptable limits.

There is a reciprocal relationship of fundamental importance here. In exchange for behavior that indicates general respect for the role of the commission as a whole, regard for colleagues, and acceptance of differences in views as flowing from different conceptions of the public interest, chairmen enjoy the "trust" of their colleagues. This trust is the basis for the discretion allowed chairmen and, overall, an impressive leadership role. Chairmen may indicate respect for the collegial arrangement by consultation, especially through sharing information, and, in general, avoiding the exclusion of others from matters in which they feel their legitimate interests to be involved. Conversely, if chairmen are perceived as placing their colleagues in a box which they might find uncomfortable or embarrassing, falling prey to the "one man band temptation," or otherwise demeaning them, trust will end, relationships will deteriorate, and the discretion and influence of chairmen will diminish. When trust is lost, a chairman's every move will be suspect to some.

The record indicates that it takes much over a considerable period for relationships within a commission to reach a point at which the natural advantages of a chairman in exercising influence are offset and his leadership becomes, in effect, an issue with which the commission is concerned. Of the twenty-six chairmen whose service essentially took place during the 1961–74 period, three and perhaps a fourth might be said to have experienced a leadership crisis. In each case, the crisis erupted after from four to eight years in office, when the chairman had served with several members for a number of years, and when there was reason to believe that a change in the chairmanship was likely.[43] The rarity of overt challenges indicates a great institutional tolerance regarding the behavior of chairmen and attests once more to the strength that inheres in the position.

8.

Regulatory Agency Governance:
A Summing Up

Two final tasks remain to be executed in this exploration of regulatory agency governance. One is to draw together in summary fashion patterns in agency governance and their underpinnings. The other is to examine the implications of patterns of governance in public policy perspective.

Patterns

In the seven agencies, agency governance may be described in terms of chairman-centered collegia. Staff and members are not without influence by any means. In important respects, however, the influence of staff on major matters is closely attached to the position of chairmen. Chairmen stand apart from other regulators in scope of activity, engagement in regulatory processes, and in imprint on regulatory determinations. In the discussion of administrative functions, chairmen were described as preeminent. That characterization might well be applied across the whole spectrum of agency enterprise, in which, as one chairman asserted, "The chairman is the key." The domain of chairmen is extensive. They have substantial influence on critical aspects of staff activity. At the commission level, they have considerable opportunity for independent action and considerable influence in collective decision-making. Their capacity to affect regulatory values and objectives—the basic stakes in agency government— is much greater than others in the commissions.

All in all, the influence of chairmen in regulatory processes may be characterized as extraordinary, placing them in a leadership position. Consequently, the commissions are not true plural executive systems. Perhaps anticipating and certainly following statutory revisions, a significant measure of integration of executive responsibility and capacity has occurred in the chairmanship. The executive dimension of chairmanships has, in fact, developed to a form much richer and more impressive than the statute-based charters imply, much less specify. Complexity and attendant necessity—especially related to increasingly hostile environments and crafting regulatory responses which are coherent in policy and program terms—have combined with the ambitions and skills of particular chairmen often enjoying presidential support in leading to the present role configuration.

The role of chairmen has two major components. One is participant in formal collective decision-making, which not uncommonly involves leadership. The other component may be designated the executive. It includes important functions in agency administration or management narrowly defined. But it also includes functions associated with overall agency management and having major substantive import, functions which fall in the gray areas which are not dealt with in formal specifications of authority and responsibility. The executive component of the chairman's role generally includes the following essential parts:

1. To decide on administrative matters.

2. To guide agency activity in an integrated fashion.

3. To direct the work of staff in behalf of the collegium.

4. To provide leadership in framing agendas and priorities.

5. To initiate and legitimize departures from the routine or established approaches to regulatory problems, and especially the formulation of underlying regulatory concepts.

6. To represent the agency to its environment and to interpret the environment to the agency.

7. To create and maintain a context and circumstances in which member roles as participants in collective decision-making can be executed successfully.

In contrast, the role component that dominates the position of member is participant in collective decision-making in formal proceedings. The executive component of the role of members is marked by some ambiguity but may be described basically in terms of ratification of decisions, advice-giving, and providing support for the initiatives and efforts of chairmen.

There are some differences in the places of chairmen in agency governance when examined comparatively. The most important and interesting ones distinguish the Federal Communications Commission and the Interstate Commerce Commission from the rest. The basis of the differences may be understood best in terms of tradition and political circumstance which have placed them at a different stage of structural development. The foundation for the emergence of a "modern" chairmanship was only laid in the Interstate Commerce Commission by the 1969 reorganization which did away with the rotational arrangement. It has yet to be laid formally in the Federal Communications Commission. More remarkable than the comparatively restrictive environment in which the chairmen of the two agencies are placed, however, is their importance and substantial influence. Despite a lag in formal redefinition, the roles of chairmen and members are not fundamentally different from those characteristic of the other agencies, and there are indications that the chairmanship is becoming more important in them. The pressures exerted on the agencies require mobilization of agency resources and development of viable policy and program responses which, in turn, require increasing measures of centralized activity. Despite the traditional constraints, chairmen in both agencies can take initiatives and adjust circumstances in order to meet the imperatives of situations, consequently adding to the importance of their positions.

The analysis has indicated that the impressive place of chairmen in agency governance rests upon several elements. One consists of the formal prerogatives of their position as spelled out in legislation, reinforced by the willingness of colleagues to accept the differential which is found in law, their perception of the chairman as the president's man, and their association of a measure of centralized authority and responsibility with administrative effectiveness. Such elements combine with the behavior of colleagues and chairmen which members experience when they join commissions to produce expectations regarding the chairmanship which are generous, though perhaps differing in particulars. The potency of the position of chairman is reinforced further by the strategic resources associated with it, especially in regard to knowledge, processes, and the products of staff activity. These resources are accentuated in importance by the complexity within and surrounding regulatory activity. All of these elements combine with the interests of members and staff to produce a high degree of receptivity to leadership emanating from the chair. On the other side, the expectations and interests of chairmen usually go in the same direction.

Thus the role of regulatory agency chairmen is complex and inclusive regarding the regulatory and support functions which occupy the agencies. The role of their colleagues is substantially less complex and more limited. The chairman's role is one in which leadership in relation to colleagues and staff is an important part and in

which a considerable capacity for independent initiatives is sanctioned.
A generous sense of the chairmanship, broadly shared, has for the most
part become a part of the institutional fabrics of the various agencies.
The impressive place of chairmen in agency governance may be characterized further as secure in its underpinnings, stable in at least broad
outline, and typically free of substantial, overt conflict. The uses of
the chair may vary with the orientations and backgrounds of incumbents, but the essential characteristics of the position do not depend
on these.

One limited circumstance in which conflict over agency governance
may arise is when formal proposals for extensive changes in systems of
governance highlight and force attention to basic questions of roles,
relationships, relative influence, and the concepts underlying the
structure and form of regulatory activity. Frontal attacks and suggestions for comprehensive alterations tap uncertainties and strain the
delicate and sensitive arrangements concerning the place of members
in the agencies. Adjustments that might be allowed to take place, even
approvingly, in evolutionary and incremental fashion may generate
heat in other forms. Particularly, members will tend to resist changes
perceived as diminishing their place in the agency. That resistance
may be overcome, as it was in certain of the 1950 and 1961 reorganization proposals, but even there some compromises were caused by
opposition.[1] Resistance may be successful, as the Federal Communications Commission and Interstate Commerce Commission cases
indicate. The more recent reorganization efforts in the Securities and
Exchange Commission and, again, in the Federal Communications
Commission, discussed in chapter 5, are further illustrations.

The members' sensitivity regarding their place in the scheme of
things, a matter which is typically central when extensive changes are
proposed, does not relate just to the role of the chairman. Indeed,
more important in this context may be relative influence of the commission level and the staff level. Members often appear to be more
fearful of enlarging the role of staff in agency governance than of
extending the role of the chairman. The major reason does not involve
the special relationship between chairmen and staffs, although that
may be a part. Chairmen, though different, are a part of the collegium. Their activities may be viewed as representative of the interests
of their colleagues in relation to the staff and in other respects. The
real rivals of members are the staff. Changes, such as the creation of a
managing director with responsibility for directing substantive staff
activities, threaten a diminution of the role of members much more
than staff direction from the office of the chairman. Ironically, then,
members may prefer systems of agency governance which accentuate
the position of chairmen in relation to the staff because rightly or

wrongly they perceive their capacity to influence chairmen as greater than their capacity to control and direct staff lead by a staff official with greater authority.

Another circumstance in which conflict may arise over agency governance is when the behavior of chairmen fails to meet the expectations of colleagues. Chairmen may take too limited a view of their role and not supply the leadership which others view as necessary. It has been noted before that very few chairmen serving in recent years have manifested that narrow sense of role which was termed the administrative. Practically all have been activist, albeit to differing degrees. A more likely source of conflict concerns matters in which colleagues have substantial participatory claims. Chairmen may take so expansive a view of their role as to project themselves as, in effect, *the* executive head of an agency and imply that the other members are impediments. But legitimation of a substantial leadership role for chairmen has not been accompanied by defining the role of colleagues only in terms of followership. The operative sense of collegiality which may be discerned in all the agencies requires chairmen to recognize continually the special place of colleagues in regulatory processes and their claim to shared responsibility in the ultimate sense. Operationally, this concept of collegiality is not a great limitation on the exercise of leadership by chairmen, but it does affect the form and processes through which chairmen may make effective use of the leadership capacities associated with the position. Collegiality requires a certain civility toward colleagues. Civility is manifested in behavior which reflects a recognition of the special place of other members and the value of their contributions to regulatory determinations. It requires allowing colleagues to have their say on matters of importance to them and informing them on matters which, if they remained ignorant, might cause discomfort or embarrassment. In simplest form, the concept of collegiality for chairmen means consult and do not demean. Civility toward colleagues earns chairmen their trust. Trust, in turn, allows chairmen considerable discretion in agency affairs and a basis for leadership in collective decisions.

The possibilities for serious, overt conflict regarding agency governance are moderated by several factors. Members tend to be political men who realize that though there may be basic agreement regarding roles and relationships, there are going to be differences. In political context, differences are handled through neglect or accommodation so that the organism can continue to function. Confrontation is avoided. Under present circumstances, substantial reformulation of the roles of chairmen and members would require highly disruptive confrontation. The interests of members on balance are best served by acceptance of present outlines, which means acceptance of the preeminence of chairmen. Tangible considerations reinforce the stylistic proclivities in handling differences associated with the term "political." Chairmen and members come and go with considerable frequency. Under ordinary circumstances, there is not time for members to develop a sense of joint interests and for individual chairmen to exhaust the patience of colleagues to the point at which arrangements for governance are challenged. It was said in the previous chapter that serious conflict about agency governance has erupted very few times. These situations had several underlying conditions in common: aggressive chairmen with very broad views of role, the prospect of their departure after a long period in their position, and a commission membership which had been fairly stable over a period of years, which allowed antagonisms to build.

Disquiet on the part of members need not always result in frontal challenges to systems of agency governance and the place of chairmen in them. Tension developing over time may result in what one former assistant designated as "the game of screw the chairman." As the game is played, the chairman's life may be complicated somewhat by heel-dragging and corridor and conference room criticism. A climate of this type has only limited implications for the characteristics of governance systems or for the chairman's place or capacities in them, as long as the game is not transformed into a concerted movement for change. One important reason why this condition exists is that the influence of chairmen depends only in part upon the quality of relationships with colleagues. Members may willingly follow chairmen even when relationships are strained at the personal level. Furthermore, chairmen have a range of resources to employ, found in their relationships outside the agency and with staff, in their capacity to shape the processes associated with regulatory activity, and in the normal prerogatives of the chair. Employing these, they may act independently, they may shape their colleagues' access to points of decision in significant ways, and they may in certain circumstances impose their positions on others.

Systems of agency governance allow chairmen to make a considerable impact on what the commissions do and how they do it. The nature and range of opportunities for impact, in relation to that of colleagues, is characterized in table 7, albeit impressionistically, in terms of the major types of decisions which have been employed in the analysis.

The characterizations underscore two important points not only regarding the place of chairmen and their colleagues but also in regard to the permeability of regulatory systems to the preferences of individuals who find themselves within them for a time. Even chairmen can affect only so much. Of particular importance, the agendas and

TABLE 7
IMPACT ON REGULATORY DECISIONS

Decisions	Impact	
	Chairmen	Members
Contextual		
Institutional Character	Substantial	Limited
Agenda	Moderate	Limited
Priorities	Substantial	Limited
Style	Moderate	Limited
Substantive Decisions of Consequence		
Formal Proceedings		
Adjudication	Substantial	Substantial
Rule-making, etc.	Substantial	Moderate
Others (e.g., positions on legislation and in negotiations)	Substantial	Moderate

the priorities which guide regulatory activity are subject to a variety of influences which agency decision-makers must recognize. The capacities of chairmen and members come more closely into balance in circumstances in which they must jointly decide, in formal proceedings. Even there, especially in non-adjudicatory proceedings, there is a difference with chairmen having substantially more weight, especially because of their ties with staff.[2]

Agency Governance and Regulatory Performance

It was noted in chapter 1 that an enduring theme in assessments of economic regulation has been a hypothesized relationship between the commission form and unsatisfactory performance. The analysis of systems of agency governance provides a basis for adding to and clarifying aspects of the debate through posing three closely related questions. First, what does the foregoing analysis suggest regarding commission arrangements as a cause of perceived limitations in regulatory performance? Second, what does it imply for the concepts of collegiality and independence in relation to the manner in which regulatory activity proceeds? Third, what does an understanding of the nature of systems of regulatory agency governance suggest regarding strategies for improving performance?

Assessments of limitations in regulatory performance were discussed previously. To recapitulate briefly, problems often have been pointed to in both the what and how in economic regulation, in both the substantive and operational dimensions of commission activity. The agencies have been taken to task for undue responsiveness to the interests of the regulated and a lack of responsiveness to the dynamics of technology and the economy. They have been criticized for failing to coordinate policy with other parts of government. Decisions are made without the right information and without articulation of the standards upon which they are based. In the operational dimension, regulatory activity is marked by delay, procedural limitations, overemphasis on adjudicatory forms, leniency in enforcement, and inadequate linkages with related programs; and overall, it is marked by the absence of a contextual set of priorities to guide effort.[3] For the Ash council as well as others, it is the commission arrangement that is at least one of the major sources of these difficulties. The "essence"— the collegial arrangement—and the "deficiencies" are "inseparable,"[4] a diagnosis based largely on the assumption that the commission form results in "multiple direction" and "splintered management."[5] A fragmented authority structure precludes the appropriate integration and direction of regulatory activity.

There are several general points to be drawn from the analysis of agency governance which are relevant for the diagnostic line emphasizing the structural sources of performance inadequacies. The structure of authority and influence within agencies is not what it is often assumed to be. It is better described in terms of a fairly high level of integration around the chairmanship, not fragmentation. Agency governance arrangements have not proved to be as resistant to change as they are often assumed to be. Instead, during the last two decades extensive adaptations, sparked by statutory revisions, changes in the environment of regulatory activity, and the actions of chairmen themselves have occurred. Systems of agency governance now possess a capacity for continuing adaptation centered in the position of chairman. Consequently, it does not seem that contending with many of the performance problems to which critics have pointed is barred by the commission form.

An examination of substantive and operational problems in relation to arrangements for agency governance suggests the possibilities which are allowed by present organizational forms. First, however, it should be emphasized that the purpose of this discussion is not to examine the validity of the varied critical assessments. There is no basis here for conclusions regarding the level of effectiveness in regulatory performance or the validity of specific critics' assertions, although some subsequent comments may bear on the issues. Rather, the purpose is to explore the relationship between agency governance and those characteristics of performance identified as problems.

Regulatory commissions are not free agents in the manner in which they operate, nor are agencies of any type. The "givens" of situations must be kept in mind when considering the ability of organizations of any type to alter the manner in which they function. For the commissions, procedure is to a major extent specified as are many substantive emphases. Much depends on the level of funds given by Congress. The nature and direction of effort are unavoidably influenced by the initiatives of the regulated. Cooperation depends as much upon those with whom relationships are to be maintained as on the commissions themselves. Within limits, however, much rests upon how the agencies wish to conduct their affairs. Obvious examples are the larger priorities which guide the allocation of resources, the adeptness with which those resources are employed, the innovativeness displayed in adjusting to new circumstances, the means employed for policy and program development, and the initiatives undertaken in relation to other agencies. In critical areas such as these, the commission form does not require that chairmen be simply *pares inter pares.* To the contrary, the working arrangements can be described as collegial only in a very general sense. The capacities of chairmen, with modest exceptions made for the Federal Communications Commission and the Interstate Commerce Commission, are probably little if any less than if they were single administrators presiding over regulatory programs. The processes through which capacity is employed may be different, but executives standing alone, too, are encumbered in their use of discretion by the views and interests of associates.

When the substance of regulatory determinations is examined, restrictive "givens" appear once again. The restrictions are, in a sense, more intractable because of their ties to politically powerful interests with stakes in regulatory determinations. But, as in the case of operational matters, there is room for choice. The collegium is more significant here but influence is not equally shared in regard to the agenda, the refinement of the agenda into priorities, the style reflected in regulatory activity, the context and basis upon which particular decisions are made—all of fundamental importance in determining the "what" of regulation. Extraordinary influence has developed in the chairmanship, or at least the capacity for it.

Collegial Decisions

The chairmanship, then, tends to be quite strong in several important aspects of agency activity. But one of the major advantages attributed to the collegial form by its defenders and even by some critics is that decisions are strengthened by presentation of a variety of perspectives and their critical examination by colleagues. Does the extraordinary influence of chairmen result in limitations on the consideration of varied points of view in agency decision-making processes, perhaps offsetting some of the positive effects of strengthening the position?

To the extent that chairmen decide independently when in former times there was the involvement of colleagues, the consideration of diverse points of view may be limited. Even in these circumstances, however, processes are not closed, and, additionally, many important matters continue to be decided by members acting together. Overall, plentiful opportunities remain for the development and expression of different points of view in decision-making processes. Indications are that no matter what the final outcome might be, in important matters there are likely to be extensive differences expressed, including differences which may have an impact on the chairman's position. It cannot be determined whether decision-making processes are any less rich in the variety and power of the perspectives that are introduced than in past times. Perhaps they are. But varied perspectives are not now absent by any means, according to several members and chairmen. Furthermore, some who came with a bias against collegial decision-making changed their position to a favorable one based upon the presence and positive effects of variety in perspectives and positions asserted. A former commissioner who served for a number of years with a chairman who employed his position to the fullest became convinced that group decision-making resulted in better decisions than if one man made the choices. He used as an example a situation in which there were differences among members regarding the amount of a rate increase, with the position of the chairman prevailing. The consequence of the participation of others appeared in the body of the decision and set out the basis of the result. In the member's view, this was of much greater long-run importance than the precise amount of the increase, and it was such questions that he focused on with some success in commission-level processes. A single decision-maker, he felt, would be tempted to gloss over the real foundations, but colleagues can at the least require specification.

It may be, however, that the bases of decisions ordinarily are not sharply and thoroughly delineated, as many critics charge. Collegial decision-making does seem to carry with it the necessity to compromise which may cloud critical aspects of choice in formal opinions. Vagaries and omissions in written products do not necessarily indicate the absence of a clash of views in antecedent processes; in fact, they may result from such clashes. But questions regarding the quality of decisions must be pursued through analyses different from that reported here. It does seem, however, that decision-making processes remain open to a considerable extent to different points of view, and in this sense there remains a collegial character to those processes.

Responsiveness, Coordination, and Accountability

The contemporary chairmanship, also contrary to characterizations of the Ash council, constitutes a linkage with the rest of government in a way that has significance for the problems of policy responsiveness, coordination, and potentially for accountability. Chairmen, as chairmen, are the president's men within limits. Just as the term *collegiality* unqualified no longer accurately describes arrangements within agencies because of the nature of the chairmanship, *independence* no longer accurately characterizes the relationship between the agencies and the executive branch, in part because of the nature of the chairmanship.

Principally through the position of chairman, the regulatory agencies stand in relatively close association with the executive branch in various important respects, rather than being truly independent of it. Presidents and their administrations have and employ a variety of means to touch and affect the commissions.[6] Contemporary studies of regulatory activity suggest a relatively high rate of interaction among agencies and other parts of the government. These plus the interviews indicate at the least a characteristic identification of agency leadership with the major orientations and themes of administrations.

The appointment of chairmen by presidents is of critical importance in the movement of commissions and other agencies into association. Chairmen are recruited and selected with an assumption that they, as chairmen, will constitute part of an administration. Chairmen accept appointment with that understanding. In recent years there has been a notable tendency for new administrations to establish their imprint on the agencies through early and comprehensive changes in chairmanships. President Gerald Ford, for example, appointed new chairmen of six of the seven agencies examined here in little more than one year after assuming office.[7] In the processes of selection, compatibility of general views regarding the nature and course of regulation seems to be of importance. Again, reports on President Ford's appointees clearly serve as an example.[8]

Consequently, chairmen typically feel an obligation to play in concert with the major themes of administration policy. One of the more sensitive and perceptive chairmen serving during recent years commented that there should be some way for the public in the larger sense to influence regulatory directions, implying that chairmen selected by a president were one important means. As a presidential appointee, he felt it quite appropriate to ensure that relevant administration policy should at the least be fully considered in agency decision-making.[9]

To what extent does the linkage of commissions with presidents, their administrations, and other parts of government through chairmen serve purposes beyond the infusion of the general orientations of an administration into regulatory determinations and facilitating coordination? Are the narrow political interests of an administration also served through affecting particular decisions? Obviously, this is a very difficult question to answer. One does not expect such matters to be discussed freely. And there are serious problems of interpretation which can only be resolved by knowing the motives of those making decisions. The generous treatment of airlines on fare questions during recent years, for example, could be interpreted in two ways: as rewarding interests who were important political supporters of Richard Nixon, or as reflecting defensible policy views regarding the appropriate means for alleviating the increased costs of the carriers and maintaining a viable air transportation system. It is not and can never be entirely clear which was the basis of decision since knowledge is lacking about what was in the minds of those who made the choices.

The reports and rumors surrounding regulatory activity in recent years contain some allegations of questionable practices on the part of chairmen, such as political fund-raising.[10] There also have been suggestions of substantial interest in particular decisions by the White House[11] and suspect political sensitivity displayed by chairmen.[12] The notable point, because of the thousands of decisions and the scores of individuals involved in making them, is that so few questionable acts have come into view, even during the last few years when public, media, and congressional interest in such matters has been unusually high.[13]

A critical area regarding partisan-motivated influences in regulatory activity concerns not crude efforts to favor a particular party or interest in a regulatory matter, but the possible politicizing of staff. Significant numbers of top staff positions are now in the noncareer executive assignment (NEA) classification. The White House routinely has a clearance function in filling them.[14] In addition, for years the

White House under Democratic and Republican administrations alike has referred prospective staff appointees to the agencies, even beyond NEA positions. Again, the answer to the question of the impact of political considerations in staff appointments is not clear. The tendency to move career staff into even NEA positions suggests it is limited. The impression derived from observing the appointment processes at work is that political affiliation, political reliability, and partisan points of view, in themselves, are not determinative. The critical criteria are competency and the notions of chairmen in regard to the perspectives in appointees which, to them, are desirable. Staff appointments may be said to have become politicized only if the term is defined to include purposefully emphasizing particular substantive orientations with policy significance in staff selection.

Kenneth Cox, a member of the Federal Communications Commission during the terms of three presidents, has said, "I have never seen evidence that the President of the United States exercised much influence over the commission on anything."[15] Others would no doubt disagree. Overall, however, on particular substantive matters the relationship between the White House and commissions seems marked by distance rather than intimacy, despite the development of extensive institutional linkages. Even on matters of policy and program significance which do not involve decisions in formal proceedings, there are limits to association. Several barriers to intimacy are of importance.

Chairmen can regulate the relationship and may maintain a certain aloofness. To share general orientations does not always lead to agreement on the specifics. To identify with a political party and a president does not necessarily lead to subservience to every proposition offered in their names. Chairmen are affected in their behavior by a host of other considerations, including the expectations of their colleagues, staff, and the Congress, and their sense of institutional interests. These quite often pull in the direction of independence, or against administration objectives and ambitions. In the interviews, chairmen generally indicated a sophisticated understanding of their place and responsibilities in this complex of relationships. There seemed to be general acceptance of a concept of independence which recognizes as legitimate certain ties and associations at the level of general policy, but which is protective of the independence of the agencies on particular matters. Further, this sense of independence is buttressed by the realization that in political terms, chairmen possess important resources that can be employed to maintain what are considered to be appropriate relationships. These include, in some instances, a sense of the dependence of the president on them in a variety of ways, ranging from acceptance of the position in the first instance to the administration of agency affairs in such a way that no political embarrassment will result.

Chairmen are also subject to the tensions playing on political officials which come from a dual and at times conflicting identification with administrations and with their own agencies. A White House staff member during the Nixon administration captured the essence when he said, referring to political executives in general, "We only see them at the annual White House Christmas party; they go off and marry the natives."[16] The representation of particular organizational interests is a familiar and potent imperative. It has much to do with the effectiveness of an official within the agency he heads. In regulatory agency context, a significant measure of independence on particular decisions is generally considered to be an important organizational interest; chairmen who do not reflect that interest in their own relations with others will compromise their leadership capacities. Agencies also have program and jurisdictional interests which chairmen, such as that of the Interstate Commerce Commission, must assert even if it means opposing administration sanctioned proposals for reorganizing the regulation of transportation.[17] It is not difficult to find other examples of chairmen taking stands contrary to positions associated with presidents and their administrations on grounds of institutional interests.[18]

The recent experience of the Ford administration in its deregulation efforts presents an interesting picture of these phenomena at work. Early in the process of conducting an organized review of economic regulation managed from the White House, all of the agency chairmen, with one exception, publically indicated their support for the critical examination. The number included several who had been appointed by President Nixon. Supposedly they were indicating support for and agreement with the general policy orientations associated with the term *deregulation.* Subsequently, several of the chairmen were succeeded by Ford appointees who purportedly were in agreement with the deregulation effort. But as the issue of deregulation has come down to specifics, to questions about withdrawals or relaxations in particular jurisdictions, agreement has begun to weaken and organizational views, understandably protective of existing regulatory arrangements though not opposed necessarily to modification, are reflected by chairmen.[19]

Chairmen, including those with philosophical and political ties with the presidents who named them, have stood apart in a variety of ways, ranging from ignoring appeals to participate in partisan fund-raising activities, to rejecting recommendations in personnel matters, to taking exception to budgetary decisions, to asserting different positions on legislative and other particular substantive questions. There is sufficient evidence of disagreement to indicate a considerable capacity for independent action. Nor does it appear that any chairman has been replaced in recent years because of the maintenance of an independent stance. Changes have come about for political reasons to be sure, principally in connection with changes in administrations and occasionally because a chairman has become a political liability or in some way has lost effectiveness,[20] but not because of too limited receptivity to administration efforts at influence.

The possibilities for intimacy are also diminished because administrations may not have policy positions on important matters that regulatory agencies decide. The chairman who reported an obligation at least to see that administration policies were considered in agency decision-making processes went on to specify a very large and significant economic area with which his agency was beginning to deal as an example of a problem in which it would be proper to use administration policy as a reference point. Unfortunately, he noted, there was no administration policy. In its comments on the Ash council report, the Federal Power Commission said:

> The crux of the problem with respect to the regulation of energy is not that regulatory activities are not coordinated with "national policy goals." Nor is the problem that the Commission form of regulation prevents effective response to industrial, technological, and economic change. The Nation's policy goals concerning the development and utilization of energy and the structural, technological, and economic problems of the energy industries are in a state of upheaval and crisis; national policy goals concerning the uses and need for energy are obscured by a panoply of conflicting problems ranging from intense environmental pressures to sensitive questions of our national security needs. It is to these much more basic and profound concerns that initial attention must be drawn rather than to the secondary issue of the best organizational structure to implement an as yet imprecisely defined national energy policy.[21]

As chairman of the Federal Power Commission, John Nassikas led the commission on the natural gas pricing issue in directions compatible with the Nixon administration's stance. In his many statements, including those before congressional committees, however, he seemed never to miss a chance to make two points: he was a very active participant in efforts within the executive branch to craft a national energy policy; at such time as there might be a national energy policy, and with each recitation he became more pessimistic about the prospect, he would be more than happy for the Federal Power Commission to be guided by its content.

In addition to the absence of policy, many issues of importance in the regulatory context are of low salience from presidential

perspective. The issues and the political stakes simply are not of the
sort to draw presidential interest, or even the interest of presidential
aides. There are also political hazards in appearing to meddle in particular matters, and thus the political interests of presidents may be best
served by avoidance rather than involvement.[22] Many times there is
nothing to gain politically from favoring one set of contending interests over another; the results could probably be scored only in terms
of ingrates and enemies. Hazards such as these are most pronounced
for presidents in formal proceedings involving rates, licenses, mergers,
and the like. Because of political dangers in behind-the-scenes participation, when the interests of an administration and other government
agencies are touched by formal proceedings, those interests increasingly are being asserted through formal and public means. For example,
the Department of Transportation is frequently a participant in formal
proceedings, and the Council on Wage and Price Stability has inter-
vened in a number of rate matters, reflecting the Ford administration's
deregulation perspective.[23]

In summary, the development of systems of agency governance
which accentuate the role of chairmen has altered but not erased the
meaning of independence as applied to the relationship between regulatory commissions and the executive branch. The chairmanship is a
means through which the agencies have and can be further brought
into concert with national policies in important economic areas and
the processes through which those policies are forged. Independence
retains meaning in two important senses. The first is in the opportunity to speak out in opposition to presidential initiatives, or the initiatives of other departments and agencies which may have presidential
sanction, when vital organizational interests are seen to be at stake.
The tradition of independence, closely associated with the commission form, allows the regulatory agencies perhaps greater opportunity
for asserting views than is the case for comparable agencies within
the executive branch proper. The second way in which independence
remains important is as a restraint on the exertion of narrow, politically based interests in agency decision-making processes.

All in all, the commission form seems no barrier to association
with other parts of government on important things, and at present
would appear to allow significant presidential influence on large
policy matters when there is coherent national policy. But guidance
does not mean control. Particularistic organizational traditions and
interests pull against full association. When presidential policy in
connection with energy, transportation, or communications, for
example, includes acceptance of the basic, relevant regulatory program outlines, the chances of serious conflict are reduced, and the

chances for adjustments in regulatory approaches and stances are enhanced via the chairmanship. It could at least be argued that under such circumstances the condition of separateness which has often been criticized no longer pertains, at least in extreme form. But when presidential initiatives involve basic changes in regulatory systems, as deregulation does, despite the contemporary chairmanship traditional agency orientations and a residual sense of independence may be asserted, although accommodations may come in the face of pressure. The resistance may be only that expected when any organization, no matter of what type, is faced with basic challenges. Efforts of agencies such as the Army Corps of Engineers and the Office of Economic Opportunity to protect themselves are not news. The difference in the case of regulatory commissions may be that traditional independence allows them to do so more aggressively, more openly, and more insistently.

The relationship between regulatory commissions, presidents, and, in a sense, the executive branch is characterized by both intimacy and distance, with the chairman in the middle. A substantial basis for coordination and cooperation is apparent. Given the ties which are possible at the policy level, it is not clear, in public policy perspective, the extent to which the residual capacity of the agencies to challenge presidential initiatives should be considered a problem. Conflicts, it has been suggested, are most likely when basic changes in regulatory systems are proposed. It may well be that the opportunity to articulate and assert a different point of view may enrich policy debates on important questions.

Regardless of the position one might develop on this matter, it is clear that systems of agency governance allow important linkages with other parts of government through the chairmanship. In these linkages, chairmen have considerable discretion. Consequently there appear to be at the most only limited structural barriers to agency responsiveness to national policy and coordination with other organizations. The barriers that exist derive most importantly, instead, from different views regarding the appropriate goals of and approaches to economic control. Further, the ties that have developed between chairmanships and the presidency, in conjunction with the leadership position of chairmen, provide a means for securing accountability in regulatory performance. That promise will be realized when presidents make more assiduous use of their capacity to appoint and dismiss chairmen on policy grounds. The potential is there and, hazarding a prediction, it may well be the next step in the evolution of the relationship between the president and the regulatory agencies.

Strategies for Improving Regulatory Performance

In chapter 1, various views about the meaning of regulatory effectiveness, how it may be evaluated, and the variables which are related
to effective performance were discussed. The Ash council report is a
prime example of the perspective in which organizational structure is
a critical, if not determinant, variable. The council saw a broad range
of undesirable consequences resulting from the commission form.
Central among these was the impossibility of the emergence of centralized, focused leadership capable of serving as a point of accountability, a stimulus for responsiveness, and means for coordination
and direction of regulatory activities. It appears, however, that regulatory agency structure has proved to be much more flexible and
adaptive than was assumed by the council. The tendency has been
for the chairmanship to develop in such a way as to be capable of
meeting many, if not all, of the requirements associated with effective regulatory program management which were specified. This suggests that the larger problems perceived in regulatory agency performance and its effects originate fundamentally in such phenomena
as the nature of the assigned responsibilities themselves, the particulars of the laws which are administered, and the politics surrounding
regulatory activity, and not in the commission form. Even in the
Federal Communications Commission, allocations of authority between the chairman and colleagues are perhaps less telling influences
on agency behavior than other factors. Certain organizational questions, such as the allocation of transportation responsibilities to three
commissions, remain at issue. This dimension of the organizational
problem was not emphasized here, but the capacity of the agencies
to coordinate their actions and a common sensitivity, if not responsiveness, to national policy to the extent it may exist, hints that such
structural features may be of limited significance. The strategic meaning of these conclusions is that approaches for improving regulatory
performance which assume the commission form to be the problem,
are not likely to achieve the desired effects. Particularly, given the
development of the position of chairman, the single-administrator
notion would seem to have little to recommend it. Alternative
strategies need to be explored.

The proper strategies to pursue regarding the large problems concerning the ends and ultimate effects of regulatory activity depend,
of course, upon the definition of those ends. If one accepts the basic
outlines of the present system of economic regulation and defines
performance problems in terms similar to those employed by the Ash
council, there remain a variety of strategic approaches which can be
used within the context of present organizational arrangements.

Specification of ways to improve performance was not one of the purposes of this analysis. Nevertheless, it might be useful to indicate several approaches which emerge from it both as specific steps that may be helpful and as illustrations of the kinds of strategies which seem suited to enhancing performance capabilities. By and large they concern the chairmanship and fundamental relationships within the agencies and between them and other parts of government. They involve fuller use of the position of chairman in ways that do not diminish the working concept of collegiality.

One promising approach concerns chairmen themselves. In order for agencies to perform effectively, chairmen must effectively perform their roles. A commission may compensate for certain inadequacies in staff and even among members. But a chairman's limitations in the role cannot really be offset. A reluctance to meet the expectations which now surround the position or a rejection of the prerogatives of the chair would cause a vacuum which could not be filled. Although restraints imposed by some colleagues and staff may impede role performance, the more likely source under present circumstances is the failure of chairmen to grasp fully the nature of that role, or their unwillingness to behave truly in accordance with its requirements. Consequently, selection processes should not just ensure that appointees are "good" men or women in the conventional sense. Chairmen should be prepared by background and in interest to exercise the broad executive responsibilities which attend the position. There would be little warrant for asserting that chairmen generally are unprepared in these respects. But it does appear that a good many have tended to concentrate on substantive problems to the neglect of agency performance viewed from the broad perspective which seems associated with effective agency operations. Manuel Cohen, once a chairman of the Securities and Exchange Commission, who took a broader interest in agency affairs than he admits, once characterized the orientation when, regarding agency administration, he told a congressional committee, "That was one area of my work that I didn't like and, frankly, did as little as I could reasonably get away with."[24]

Another strategic approach concerns the relationship between chairmen and colleagues and involves giving explicit attention to those relationships, an activity in which commissions almost never engage. To do so would perhaps strengthen agency performance by making fuller use of the skills and expertise of the membership across a wide range of agency activities, reducing tension which may develop regarding roles, and preventing serious conflict from developing. Although a chairman's inclinations and performance are of basic importance in agency management and have large implications for agency effectiveness, his colleagues are not without responsibility or effect. In a very real sense, their place in agency governance is that which is masked by ambiguity, not that of chairmen. It may very well be that in more instances than not, it is their disengagement from certain areas of agency activity rather than their engagement that constitutes a negative force and thus impedes performance. One of the major difficulties is finding that delicate balance point at which the members generally are engaged in the large questions in a positive way, but without constricting the chairman in caring for his essential functions. There are no magic formulas for locating the balance. The evidence suggests, however, that the commissions almost never give systematic and focused attention to questions of balance, roles, and the quality of the working relationship between members and chairmen. In most of the agencies, the formal delineations of authority are imprecise. Even when definition has been attempted, substantial gray areas have been left. Various unsuccessful attempts to involve members of the commissions in processes beyond formal proceedings have been alluded to. Generally, these have been conceived out of the perceptions of others regarding the interests of members, rather than on the basis of specifications of members about those interests. Members have rarely if ever explored with one another the nature of their interests in matters in which they are not generally involved, or their place in agency governance. When questions have arisen, they have usually concerned particular decisions already made, not roles and allocations of responsibilities. Fundamental agreement about roles does not preclude the development of tension, carrying with it the possibility of serious conflict.

It is interesting that in settings where the working relationships between members and chairmen are so delicate and important, they are rarely dealt with directly. When members are aggravated regarding the conduct of the chairmanship, they generally refrain from raising the issue. Under present circumstances, it is really only chairmen who may open discussion on such sensitive points, yet they practically never do. It might be useful if means and periodic opportunities were provided for commission members to address questions of governance, with the support and participation of chairmen, as a way to determine how members wish to be involved and for resolving submerged differences.

Still another useful approach concerns the development of innovative ways to handle regulatory tasks. It does not take long immersion in regulatory agency activities to be struck by how little the technology associated with regulatory programs has changed over the years and how little attention is given to new ways for approaching regulatory responsibilities and executing them. Imaginative attention needs to be given to the development of alternative means for achieving regulatory objectives. Efforts by the agencies themselves are potentially among the most promising, because of their understanding and grasp of problems. Under normal circumstances prospects are limited by organizational inertia and the magnitude of the creative task, one which transcends the responsibilities and overwhelms the resources of individual agencies. Cooperative efforts would seem useful. At present, however, there is little joint attention or even conversation across agency lines on common problems. Stimulation and leadership are required, and again chairmen are in the critical position. It is only through chairmen that useful cooperative efforts could be instituted. And it is only with the support of chairmen that alterations could be made.

A final approach to pursue concerns the processes through which regulatory agency activity is linked to other parts of government. A rather haphazard pattern of interaction has grown up in which chairmen are centrally involved. Processes tend to be ad hoc and poorly understood. They are vulnerable to questions regarding their legitimacy, not so much because of doubt regarding the propriety of joint involvement in general terms, but from lack of specification regarding appropriate boundaries distinguishing matters in which the agencies should act independently from those in which cooperation is in order. The suspicion-ridden and often contentious relationship between the Federal Communications Commission and the Office of Telecommunications Policy in recent years on matters that were, simultaneously, of national policy significance and in which the agency had substantial decisional responsibilities is a clear example of the problem. Another interesting illustration which suggests the changing relationship between the agencies and the executive branch and the lack of systemization is President Ford's meeting with the chairmen of ten regulatory agencies on his deregulation program in 1975, reportedly the first time a policy discussion of this type had been held in the White House. Agency chairmen have gone to the White House many times before on various matters, but most often very quietly because of uncertainties about repercussions. It would seem reasonable and useful at this point for the linkages between the agencies and other parts of government and associated processes to be systematized as a means for eradicating uncertainties and enhancing the development and application of coherent national policy.

These suggestions grow out of an examination of seven commissions and do not exhaust the list of problems which occur across the regulatory spectrum or possible remedial approaches. They and the analysis to which they relate do point, however, to the complex, subtle nature of many impediments to agency performance and the need for remedial approaches which are appropriately complex, subtle, and based upon close analysis of regulatory processes. Organization may affect performance, and in other contexts may be a source of basic difficulties and a legitimate focus of attention in public policy perspective. But in these seven commissions, systems of governance have developed so that the commission form is not a barrier to achieving performance aims, such as those put forth by the Ash council, or to achieving the diverse objectives sought in economic regulation.

Notes

CHAPTER 1.
Introduction

1. For examples of critiques from the economist's perspective, see: Stephen G. Breyer and Paul W. MacAvoy, *Energy Regulation by the Federal Power Commission* (Washington, D.C.: The Brookings Institution, 1974); Keith C. Brown, *Regulation of the Natural Gas Producing Industry* (Washington, D.C.: Resources for the Future, Inc., 1972); William M. Capron, ed., *Technological Change in Regulated Industries* (Washington, D.C.: The Brookings Institution, 1971); George W. Douglas and James C. Miller III, *Economic Regulation of Domestic Air Transport* (Washington, D.C.: The Brookings Institution, 1974); Roger G. Noll, *Reforming Regulation: An Evaluation of the Ash Council Proposals* (Washington, D.C.: The Brookings Institution, 1971); Roger G. Noll, Merton J. Peck, and John J. McGowan, *Economic Aspects of Television Regulation* (Washington, D.C.: The Brookings Institution, 1973); and Almarin Phillips, ed., *Promoting Competition in Regulated Markets* (Washington, D.C.: The Brookings Institution, 1975).

2. The origins of the relationship between Congress and the commissions are discussed in James E. Anderson, *Emergence of the Modern Regulatory State* (Washington, D.C.: Public Affairs Press, 1962); Marver H. Bernstein, *Regulating Business by Independent Commission* (Princeton: Princeton Univ. Press, 1955), especially chap. 1; and Robert E. Cushman, *The Independent Regulatory Commissions* (New York: Oxford Univ. Press, 1941), especially pp. 448–61.

3. Congressional statements remain replete with allusions to a special relationship between Congress and the commissions. A recent manifestation of some interest is Senator Lee Metcalf's proposed "Regulatory Commissions' Independence Act," introduced in 1973. The text of the bill and other relevant material are found in, Subcommittee on Budgeting, Management, and Expenditures, Senate Committee on Government Operations, *Regulatory Commissions' Independence Act, S. 704: Compendium of Materials,* 93d Cong., 2d sess., 1974, Committee Print.

4. The provisions do not prevent presidents from naming political independents to minority positions or naming minority members generally supportive of an administration's orientations.

5. For specification of what is clear and what is not clear regarding the president's removal authority, see Emmette S. Redford, "The President and the Regulatory Commissions," *Texas Law Review* 44 (Dec. 1965), p. 288.

6. David M. Welborn, "Presidents, Regulatory Commissioners and Regulatory Policy," *Journal of Public Law* 15, no. 1 (1966), pp. 4–7.

7. The Federal Power Act provided in original form that the chairman selected by his colleagues would continue to serve as chairman "until the expiration of his term of office." In 1961, when President John F. Kennedy sought to name a new chairman, the incumbent,

Jerome Kuykendall, argued that the reorganization plan of 1950 simply transferred the authority to appoint from the commission to the President and did not alter tenure conditions. Ultimately, the controversy ended when Kuykendall stepped aside. Although the issue has never been resolved definitively, there is a basis for asserting that the reorganization plan was not simply a "conveyance." It was legislation. And the special characteristics associated with the concept of presidential designation support an interpretation that the chairman of the Federal Power Commission now serves at the pleasure of the president. Richard K. Berg to Frank M. Wozencraft, "Tenure of Chairmen of Various Commissions and Agencies," working paper, Office of Legal Counsel, Department of Justice, Jan. 6, 1969.

The situation regarding the Civil Aeronautics Board is a bit more complex. The Federal Aviation Act provides that annually the president shall appoint a member to serve as chairman of the board. The question is whether the provision precludes removal by presidential action before expiration of the term for which a chairman has been appointed. Legal arguments with some merit can be constructed on both sides of the issue. There has been no open conflict on the matter, although the potential has existed. In late 1960, Whitney Gillilland was named to serve as chairman during 1961 by President Dwight D. Eisenhower. But in February 1961, President Kennedy appointed Alan Boyd, already a member, to serve as chairman during that year. The transition from Gillilland to Boyd took place without controversy. An awkwardness was also apparent in the 1968–69 period. President Lyndon B. Johnson named John Crooker to continue as chairman for 1969. Crooker remained in office until September, then resigned, allowing a Nixon appointee to assume the position. There are indications that the new administration was discomfited by the chairman's willingness to continue through 1969, but was reluctant to press the issue.

8. On the relationships between presidents and the commissions, see Bernstein, *Regulating Business by Independent Commission,* pp. 109–13 and 126–54; Cushman, *The Independent Regulatory Commissions,* pp. 461–67 and 680–91; Redford, "The President and the Regulatory Commissions"; and Hugh M. Hall, Jr., "Responsibility of President and Congress for Regulatory Policy Development," *Law and Contemporary Problems* 26 (Spring 1961), p. 261.

9. "Views of the Administrative Conference of the United States on the 'Report on Selected Independent Regulatory Agencies' of the President's Council on Executive Organization," *Virginia Law Review* 57 (Sept. 1971), p. 928.

10. Commission on Organization of the Executive Branch of the Government, *Task Force Report on Regulatory Commissions,* app. N (Washington, D.C.: U.S. Government Printing Office, 1949), p. 21.

11. The critical commentaries on regulatory agency performance are far too numerous to cite comprehensively. A number of the works already referred to are important in this regard. Others of particular significance include: Philip Elman, "Administrative Reform of the Federal Trade Commission," *The Georgetown Law Journal* 59 (Mar. 1971), p. 777; Henry J. Friendly, *The Federal Administrative Agencies: The Need for Better Definition of Standards* (Cambridge, Mass.: Harvard Univ. Press, 1962); Louis J. Hector, "Problems of the CAB and the Independent Regulatory Commissions," *The Yale Law Journal* 69 (May 1960), p. 931; Nicholas Johnson, "A New Fidelity to the Regulatory Ideal," *The Georgetown Law Journal* 59 (Mar. 1971), p. 869; James M. Landis, *Report on Regulatory Agencies to the President-elect,* Senate Committee on the Judiciary, 86th Cong., 2d sess., 1960. Committee Print; Paul W. MacAvoy, ed., *The Crisis of the Regulatory Commissions* (New York: Norton, 1970); John E. Moore, "Recycling the Regulatory Agencies," *Public Administration Review* 32 (July/Aug. 1972), p. 291; and James Q. Wilson, "The Dead Hand of Regulation," *The Public Interest,* no. 25 (Fall 1971), p. 39.

12. In this view, as Richard A. Posner has suggested, "the typical regulatory agency operates with reasonable efficiency to attain deliberately inefficient or inequitable goals set

by the legislature that created it." "Theories of Economic Regulation, *The Bell Journal of Economics and Management Science* 5 (Autumn 1974), p. 337. The general perspective is reflected in George J. Stigler, *The Citizen and the State: Essays on Regulation* (Chicago: Univ. of Chicago Press, 1975). For an empirical analysis which explains what many economists have viewed as an outstanding example of inefficiency in regulatory context as resulting from congressional requirements, see Alan Stone, "The F.T.C. and Advertising Regulation: An Examination of Agency Failure," *Public Policy* 21 (Spring 1973), p. 203.

13. Roger C. Cramton, "Regulatory Structure and Regulatory Performance: A Critique of the Ash Council Report," *Public Administration Review* 32 (July/Aug. 1972), p. 286.

14. See Louis L. Jaffe, "The Illusion of the Ideal Administration," *Harvard Law Review* 86 (May 1973), p. 1183.

15. Noll, *Reforming Regulation: An Evaluation of the Ash Council Proposals,* p. 40.

16. Particularly interesting insights regarding politics and regulatory administration are contained in Michael E. Porter and Jeffrey F. Sagansky, "Information, Politics, and Economic Analysis: The Regulatory Decision Process in the Air Freight Cases," *Public Policy* 24 (Spring 1976), p. 263; and James Q. Wilson, "The Politics of Regulation," in James W. McKie, ed., *Social Responsibility and the Business Predicament* (Washington, D.C.: The Brookings Institution, 1974), p. 135, and especially pp. 152–68.

17. The discussion of the incentive structures of regulators in the works of Posner and Stigler, cited in n. 12, above, are also relevant here.

18. Bernstein, *Regulating Business by Independent Commission,* p. 173.

19. Major examples of assessments which place considerable emphasis on organization for economic regulation as an important determinant of regulatory performance include: The President's Committee on Administrative Management, *Report of the Committee with Studies of Administrative Management in the Federal Government* (Washington, D.C.: U.S. Government Printing Office, 1937); U.S. Commission on Organization of the Executive Branch of the Government, *Task Force Report on Regulatory Commissions,* 1949; the Hoover Commission's own assessment, *The Independent Regulatory Commissions,* Report No. 12 (Washington, D.C.: U.S. Government Printing Office, 1949); and Landis, *Report on Regulatory Agencies to the President-elect,* 1960.

20. The President's Advisory Council on Executive Organization, *A New Regulatory Framework: Report on Selected Independent Regulatory Agencies* (Washington, D.C.: U.S. Government Printing Office, 1971), p. 4.

21. *Ibid.*

22. *Ibid.*

23. The agencies to be headed by a single administrator and to be responsible to the president were the Transportation Regulatory Agency, Federal Power Agency, Securities and Exchange Agency, and the Federal Trade Practices Agency. The independent status of the Federal Communications Commission was to be retained, but its membership was to be reduced to five. A Federal Antitrust Board was to be created to assume responsibility for the antitrust jurisdiction of the Federal Trade Commission. An Administrative Court of the United States was to be established, to which appeals from certain agency decisions would go. *Ibid.,* pp. 5–7.

24. *Ibid.,* p. 34.

25. *Ibid.*

26. *Ibid.,* p. 40.

27. *Ibid.,* p. 42.

28. *Ibid.,* p. 36.

29. Glen O. Robinson, "Reorganizing the Independent Regulatory Agencies," *Virginia Law Review,* vol. 57 (Sept. 1971), p. 960.

30. The President's Advisory Council on Executive Organization, *A New Regulatory Framework,* pp. 35–36.

31. *Ibid.,* p. 36.
32. *Ibid.,* p. 37.
33. *Ibid.,* p. 38.
34. *Ibid.,* p. 39.
35. *Ibid.,* p. 38.
36. *Ibid.,* p. 33.
37. For examples of discussions of contrary views, see, for example: Cramton, "Regulatory Structure and Regulatory Performance: A Critique of the Ash Council Report"; and Noll, *Reforming Regulation: An Evaluation of the Ash Council Proposals.* Similar perspectives are set out in "Symposium on Federal Regulatory Agencies: A Response to the Ash Report," *Virginia Law Review* 57 (Sept. 1971), pp. 925–1108.

CHAPTER 2.
Agency Governance in Analytical Perspective

1. Analyses suggestive of the approach include: William L. Cary, *Politics and the Regulatory Agencies* (New York: McGraw-Hill, 1967); Edward F. Cox, Robert G. Fellmeth, and John E. Schulz, *"The Nader Report" on the Federal Trade Commission* (New York: Richard W. Baron, 1969); Robert Fellmeth, *The Interstate Commerce Omission* (New York: Grossman Publishers, 1970); A. Lee Fritschler, *Smoking and Politics: Policymaking and the Federal Bureaucracy* (New York: Appleton, 1969); Erwin G. Krasnow and Lawrence D. Longley, *The Politics of Broadcast Regulation* (New York: St. Martin's, 1973); Mark V. Nadel, *The Politics of Consumer Protection* (Indianapolis: Bobbs-Merrill, 1971); Sherman J. Maisel, *Managing the Dollar* (New York: Norton, 1973); Joseph C. Palamountain, Jr., "The Federal Trade Commission and the Indiana Standard Case," in Edwin A. Bock, ed., *Government Regulation of Business: A Casebook* (Englewood Cliffs, N.J.: Prentice-Hall, 1965), p. 156; and Emmette S. Redford, *The Regulatory Process: With Illustrations from Commercial Aviation* (Austin: Univ. of Texas Press, 1969).

2. Studies of the dynamics of regulatory processes within agencies are quite limited in scope, typically focusing on a single agency or a limited portion of a single agency's activities. Examination of a number of agencies as attempted here makes the analysis to follow somewhat distinctive. The effort is stimulated by the long-recognized but seldom satisfied need for broadly conceived empirical analyses of regulatory processes. The need for empirical analysis as a basis for dealing with questions regarding the conditions which facilitate effective regulatory performance has been recognized for years. Marver H. Bernstein, especially, has made the case powerfully in, for example, "The Regulatory Process: A Framework for Analysis," *Law and Contemporary Problems* 26 (Spring 1961), p. 329; and "Independent Regulatory Agencies: A Perspective on Their Reform," *The Annals of the American Academy of Political and Social Science* 400 (Mar. 1972), p. 14. See also, Norman C. Thomas, "Politics, Structure and Personnel in Administrative Regulation," *Virginia Law Review* 57 (Sept. 1971), p. 1033.

3. Redford, *The Regulatory Process: With Illustrations from Commercial Aviation,* pp. 22–38.

4. Welborn, "Presidents, Regulatory Commissioners and Regulatory Policy," pp. 13–28.

5. Elman, "Administrative Reform of the Federal Trade Commission," p. 785.

6. Senate Committee on Commerce, *Hearings, Natural Gas Production and Conservation Act of 1974,* 93d Cong., 2d sess., 1974, p. 93.

7. See the material contained in Subcommittee on Intergovernmental Relations, Senate Committee on Government Operations, *Hearings, Regulatory Agency Budgets,* 92d Cong., 2d sess., 1972.

8. Nondecisions at such points, of course, are quite significant.

9. Ernest Gellhorn, "Adverse Publicity by Administrative Agencies," *Harvard Law Review* 86 (June 1973), p. 1380.

10. Philip Selznick, *Leadership in Administration: A Sociological Interpretation* (Evanston, Ill.: Row, Peterson and Company, 1957), p. 35.

11. *Ibid.*, pp. 35–36.

12. Louis L. Jaffe's discussion of the Federal Communications Commission is generally suggestive. "The Illusion of the Ideal Administration," pp. 1191–97.

13. This formulation owes a good bit to the perspective found in Harold D. Lasswell and Abraham Kaplan, *Power and Society: A Framework for Political Inquiry* (New Haven: Yale Univ. Press, 1950).

14. Friendly, *The Federal Administrative Agencies,* p. 2.

15. Chester I. Barnard, *The Functions of the Executive* (Cambridge, Mass.: Harvard Univ. Press, 1968), p. 232.

16. *Ibid.*

17. The basic statutory provisions are as follows: Civil Aeronautics Board, Reorganization Plan No. 13 of 1950, 64 *Stat.* 1266; Federal Communications Commission, Communications Act, 47 *U.S.C.* 155; Federal Maritime Commission, Reorganization Plan No. 6 of 1949, 63 *Stat.* 1069, carried forward in Reorganization Plan No. 7 of 1961, 78 *Stat.* 425; Federal Power Commission, Reorganization Plan No. 9 of 1950, 64 *Stat.* 1265; Federal Trade Commission, Reorganization Plan No. 8 of 1950, 64 *Stat.* 1265; Interstate Commerce Commission, Reorganization Plan No. 1 of 1969, 83 *Stat.* 859; Securities and Exchange Commission, Reorganization Plan No. 10 of 1950, 64 *Stat.* 1265.

Agency elaborations are as follows: Civil Aeronautics Board, *C.A.B. Manual,* 1971; Federal Communications Commission, *Rules and Regulations,* 1971, and "Order Defining the Executive Responsibility of the Chairman with Respect to the Internal Affairs of the Commission," 1956; Federal Maritime Commission, *Manual of Orders,* 1973; Federal Power Commission, *Administrative Manual,* 1959; Federal Trade Commission, *Organization, Procedures and Rules of Practice,* 1971; and Interstate Commerce Commission, *Organization Minutes,* 1965.

18. Information regarding organizational patterns is drawn from descriptions contained in annual reports and various organization manuals.

19. The position of executive or managing director, another result of prior reform efforts, is well established in the agencies. These officials supervise relatively large staffs concerned with support functions. The percentage of total agency staff directly subject to their supervision ranged from 10.4 in the Interstate Commerce Commission to 17.9 in the Federal Power Commission in fiscal year 1972, according to agency budgets.

20. Discussions of the closely associated concepts of power, authority and influence are legion. The following are illustrative of contemporary perspectives: David V. J. Bell, *Power, Influence, and Authority: An Essay in Political Linguistics* (New York: Oxford Univ. Press, 1975); Dorwin Cartwright, "Influence, Leadership, Control," in James G. March, ed., *Handbook of Organizations* (Chicago: Rand McNally, 1965), p. 1; Fred E. Fiedler, *A Theory of Leadership Effectiveness* (New York: McGraw-Hill, 1967); Edwin P. Hollander and James W. Julian, "Studies in Leader Legitimacy, Influence, and Innovation," in Leonard Berkowitz, ed., *Advances in Experimental Social Psychology,* vol. 5 (New York and London: Academic Press, 1970), p. 33; and Andrew S. McFarland, *Power and Leadership in Pluralist Systems* (Stanford: Stanford Univ. Press, 1969).

21. McFarland, *Power and Leadership in Pluralist Systems,* p. 154.

22. This rationale is borrowed from John F. Manley, "Wilbur D. Mills: A Study in Congressional Influence," *American Political Science Review* 63 (June 1969), p. 442.

23. The formulation is an adaptation of French's and Raven's power-base categories. John R. P. French and Bertram Raven, "The Bases of Social Power," in Dorwin Cartwright, ed., *Studies in Social Power* (Ann Arbor: Univ. of Michigan Press, 1959), p. 150.

24. See Bruce J. Biddle and Edwin J. Thomas, eds., *Role Theory: Concepts and Research* (New York: John Wiley and Sons, 1966); Neal Gross, Ward S. Mason, and Alexander W. McEachern, *Explorations in Role Analysis: Studies of the School Superintendency Role* (New York: John Wiley and Sons, 1958); Richard C. Hodgson, Daniel J. Levinson, and Abraham Zaleznik, *The Executive Role Constellation: An Analysis of Personality and Role Relations in Management* (Boston: Division of Research, Graduate School of Business Administration, Harvard Univ., 1965); Daniel Katz and Robert L. Kahn, *The Social Psychology of Organizations* (New York: John Wiley and Sons, 1966); and John C. Wahlke, Heinz Eulau, William Buchanan, and Leroy C. Ferguson, *The Legislative System: Explorations in Legislative Behavior* (New York: John Wiley and Sons, 1962).

25. In this connection, the notion of "contingent dependencies," real and perceived, created by the necessity of coping with uncertainty, workflow centrality and nonsubstitutability as shaping the allocation of power within organizations is developed in C. R. Hinings *et al.,* "Structural Conditions of Intraorganizational Power," *Administrative Science Quarterly* 19 (Mar. 1974), p. 22.

26. On leadership in group contexts see James David Barber, *Power in Committees: An Experiment in the Governmental Process* (Chicago: Rand McNally, 1966); Barry E. Collins and Harold Guetzkow, *A Social Psychology of Group Processes for Decision-Making* (New York: John Wiley and Sons, 1964); David J. Danelski, "The Influence of the Chief Justice in the Decisional Process," in Raymond E. Wolfinger, ed., *Readings in American Political Behavior,* 2d ed. (Englewood Cliffs, N.J.: Prentice-Hall, 1970), p. 185; Robert T. Golembiewski, "Small Groups and Large Organizations," in March, ed., *Handbook of Organizations,* p. 87; Peter B. Read, "Source of Authority and the Legitimation of Leadership in Small Groups," *Sociometry* 37 (June 1974), p. 189; S. Sidney Ulmer, *Courts as Small and Not So Small Groups* (New York: General Learning Press, 1971); and Sidney Verba, *Small Groups and Political Behavior: A Study of Leadership* (Princeton: Princeton Univ. Press, 1961).

CHAPTER 3.
Chairmen, Commissioners and Agency Administration: An Overview

1. Miles W. Kirkpatrick, "Dinner Address," *Antitrust Law Journal* 40, no. 2 (1971), p. 332.

2. The characterizations in the table are syntheses of responses to a number of questions posed in the interviews.

3. Philip Elman, who challenged the agency chairman from time to time during this period, has noted in confirmation, "The other members of the Commission have not been permitted to exercise the reciprocal powers, or 'checks and balances,' vested in them under the reorganization plan." "Administrative Reform of the Federal Trade Commission," p. 857.

4. Bruce E. Thorp, "Transportation Report/Carrier Support for Status quo Helps ICC Resist Pressures for Major Overhaul," *National Journal,* Jan. 27, 1973, p. 111.

5. More than that, chairmen, despite the year's limitation on their tenure during the 1960s, were able to undertake a substantial number of initiatives. Organizational and procedural arrangements were reworked in a fairly thorough fashion. In part this was owing to the external pressure the agency was under. Changes were also facilitated by a succession of chairmen over a number of years who seemingly had the same general perspective on the agency and its problems.

6. The Federal Communications Commission is a partial exception. A reorganization plan to strengthen the chairmanship was defeated in Congress in 1961. The views of members at that time are expressed in Senate Committee on Government Operations, *Hearings,*

S. Res. 142, 143, 147, and 148 (Plan Nos. 1–5), 87th Cong., 1st sess., 1961, pp. 61–78.

7. Chairmen generally leave commissions when they cease to be chairmen. When they do remain as members, as in the cases of Whitney Gillilland of the Civil Aeronautics Board and Paul Rand Dixon of the Federal Trade Commission, indications are that they support a broad interpretation of the prerogatives of the chair among the members.

8. Large-scale turnovers in commission membership tend to come during changes in administrations. In this connection, see Welborn, "Presidents, Regulatory Commissioners and Regulatory Policy," pp. 4–7; "GOP Will Control 9 Regulatory Agencies by 1972," *Congressional Quarterly Weekly Report,* Dec. 12, 1969, p. 2577; and "Nixon Legacy: Many Long-term Appointments," *Congressional Quarterly Weekly Report,* Aug. 24, 1974, p. 2281. Extensive transformations at these times seem to enlarge the opportunities of chairmen for leadership, especially in administrative and management matters.

The general relationship between turnover rates and the influence of chairmen is a complex one. During the period under examination, the pattern in most agencies seemed to be for a significant number of those who were appointed at the start of an administration to continue for a number of years. One or a few of the positions were subject to more frequent turnover, although even in these, tenure might and generally did run to several years. A quick comparison of turnover patterns and the potency of chairmen does not indicate that length of tenure of members alone affects the capacity of chairmen in major ways. That is, stability in membership does not seem to result in significant constraints on the chair, even when the chairman is new. Nor is extensive turnover always associated with enlarged influence in the chair. However, the brand new member, who may often be present, may be somewhat more inclined than the others to defer to the chairman. Also, over a long period of time, small differences between chairmen and members may combine and grow into large ones, thus providing a basis for serious conflict. In the case of the Federal Trade Commission, for example, there was great stability in membership during the 1960s. But it was only in 1969 that the members challenged the leadership of the chairman, Paul Rand Dixon, in a direct fashion.

For additional discussion of tenure and turnover on the commissions, see: David T. Stanley, Dean E. Mann, and Jameson W. Doig, *Men Who Govern: A Biographical Profile of Federal Political Executives* (Washington, D.C.: The Brookings Institution, 1967), pp. 68–72; and Thomas, "Politics, Structure and Personnel in Administrative Regulation," p. 1033.

9. By and large, assistants to members do not seem to have significant interests in matters beyond the flow of cases. In the Federal Communications Commission, however, assistants to members have interests in agency management that are similar to those of members. Some expect assistants to chairmen to consult with them regarding activities centered in the chairman's office.

10. Nicholas Johnson and John Jay Dystel, "A Day in the Life: The Federal Communications Commission," *The Yale Law Journal* 82 (July 1973), p. 1577.

11. These are the only two agencies in which members have special, continuing responsibilities with management overtones. In the Interstate Commerce Commission, the major reflection is in the allocation of much of the decisional work among three divisions, each made up of three members, with the senior member generally serving as chairman. In the Federal Communications Commission, delegations of authority have been made to the Telegraph Committee, the Telephone Committee, and to the Subscription Television Committee. One member is also designated as the Defense Commissioner, with special responsibilities in that area. From time to time, authority may be delegated to individuals or groups of commissioners in other matters. Federal Communications Commission, *Rules and Regulations,* Part C, "Commission Organization," Subpart B, secs. 0.214–0.218, p. 26.

12. Jack Donald Edwards, "Role Concepts of Federal Regulatory Officials" (Ph.D. diss., Vanderbilt Univ., 1966), p. 102.

13. *Ibid.*, p. 105.

CHAPTER 4.
Organizational Resources

1. From the files of the Civil Service Commission.

2. Federal Power Commission, *Administrative Manual,* Sec. 6(b), p. 3. Dated Jan. 27, 1959.

3. From the files of the Civil Service Commission.

4. *Ibid.*

5. Although questions regarding appointment authority were serious and considered so by all concerned, it was not personnel issues, basically, that were involved. One of those members who raised the issue said: "The personnel issue was essentially a way of reflecting opinions about the general state of things. It was a vote of no confidence in the chairman." For a discussion of the more basic problems, see Subcommittee on Administrative Practice and Procedure, Senate Committee on the Judiciary, *Hearings, Federal Trade Commission Procedures,* 91st Cong., 1st sess., 1969. For additional details, see Elman, "Administrative Reform of the Federal Trade Commission," pp. 857–58.

6. It is not clear whether the differences were resolved by formal decision of the commission or through informal adjustment.

7. The major analyses were: American Bar Association Commission to Study the Federal Trade Commission, *Report* (1969); and Cox, Fellmeth, and Schulz, *"The Nader Report."*

8. Carole Shifrin, "A Changed FTC Stands at Policy Crossroads," *Washington Post,* Dec. 13, 1972, p. D14. Other chairmen have also devoted energy to staffing. For example, Earl Kintner, when chairman of the Federal Trade Commission, gave extensive personal attention to the recruitment of young lawyers to the agency. When chairman of the Federal Power Commission, Joseph Swidler, was continually on the look-out for talent, whether there was a precise position fitting the qualifications of the talent discovered or not. And he personally interviewed all potential appointees for positions at roughly the GS-7 level and up. Federal Maritime Commission Chairman Helen Delich Bentley interviewed prospects down to the GS-11 level, especially for legal positions.

9. In the case of one recent and important appointment, a member estimated that if there had been an unfettered vote, the vote of the members present would have been four to three in favor of approval. Instead, the approval was unanimous. "Members," according to him, "see which way the wind is blowing and won't oppose the chairman."

10. Some staff appointments made during the Eisenhower administration apparently reinforced this concern.

11. The wide discretion allowed chairmen is illustrated by a situation occurring shortly after Bradford Cook resigned the Securities and Exchange Commission chair in May, 1973. The position of general counsel had been vacant since August 1972. Shortly before he resigned, Cook had decided upon an appointment after interviewing the prospect and indicating to him that, in effect, the job was his. At this point, the commission had not been involved in the process. Two days after Cook's resignation, he contacted Commissioner Hugh F. Owens, who was acting as chairman, informed him of the situation, and gave him the material on the prospective appointee. Owens then contacted the other members and they took a position of affirmation, or nonobjection on the selection, thus concluding the matter. Owens stated, "No formal action of the Commission or minute to that effect was taken because we considered the action as more or less not only a nonobjection but an affirmation of an action taken by the former Chairman pursuant to his prerogatives prior to his resignation." Subcommittee on Commerce and Finance, House Committee on Interstate and Foreign Commerce, *Hearings, Securities and Exchange Act Amendments of 1973,* pt. 1, 93d Cong., 1st sess., 1973, pp. 397–98.

12. On the importance attached to top staff selection by Lewis Engman of the Federal Trade Commission and John Robson of the Civil Aeronautics Board, two recent chairmen,

see James W. Singer, "Regulatory Report/FTC Stresses Antitrust Effort as Weapon in Battle Against Inflation," *National Journal*, Oct. 19, 1974, p. 1568; and Richard E. Cohen, "Regulatory Report/CAB's New Chairman Charts an Independent Course," *National Journal*, Nov. 15, 1975, p. 1560.

13. Subcommittee on Commerce and Finance, House Committee on Interstate and Foreign Commerce, *Hearings, Securities and Exchange Act Amendments of 1973*, pt. 1, 1973, p. 230.

14. 5 *C.F.R.* 305.601(b).

15. The method of selecting persons to fill NEA positions recently became an issue when the chairman of the Consumer Product Safety Commission objected to White House review of prospective appointees. The controversy is capsulated in Senate Committee on Government Operations, *Hearings, Regulatory Reform—1974*, pt. 1, 93d Cong., 2d sess., 1974, pp. 86–87.

16. There are also a number of Schedule C positions in each agency. By and large, they are lower level positions in the offices of the members, essentially secretaries.

17. The Federal Maritime Commission was created in its present form in 1961 and, in this sense, all top staff officials were appointed at this time.

18. Changes in chairmanships associated with the transition from a Nixon to a Ford administration were accompanied by extensive changes in top-level staff. See, for example, Louis M. Kohlmeier's reports in the *National Journal*, such as, "CAB Illustrates Trials of Reform," Jan. 25, 1975, p. 148; and "Expiring Terms Immobilizing FPC," Apr. 5, 1975, p. 517.

19. There are indications that Chairman Swidler of the Federal Power Commission did not make a change in the executive directorship because of the assistance the incumbent had given him during the awkward period when Jerome Kuykendall was refusing to step aside.

20. Subcommittee on Intergovernmental Relations, Senate Committee on Government Operations, *Hearings, Regulatory Agency Budgets*, 1972.

21. Bruce E. Thorp, "Communications Report/FCC's Ability to Regulate AT&T Faces Test in Upcoming Investigation," *National Journal*, Mar. 11, 1972, p. 432.

22. For several years the Interstate Commerce Commission has been concerned about the relationship between holding companies and the transportation firms, especially railroads, controlled by them and with the possibility that parent firms draw off resources of operating units. More than suspicion is necessary as a basis for policy and action. Evidence is required. Prior to 1971, no finance or holding company audits were being performed, making it impossible for the agency to do more than speculate about relationships. After 1971, budgetary adjustments were made, and shortly thereafter more than 100 audits were underway. Subcommittee on Budgeting Management and Expenditures, Senate Committee on Government Operations, *Regulatory Commissions' Independence Act, S. 704: Compendium of Materials*, 93d Cong., 2d sess., 1974, p. 104. Committee Print.

23. In 1976, the agency's investigation of the petroleum industry was expected to require 18 lawyers, support staff, and the expenditure of $2.5 million. Carole Shifrin, "Engman Backs Funds Rise," *Washington Post*, June 12, 1975, p. D13.

24. The one major exception to these generalizations regarding the role of the chairman in the budget preparation process and the characterization of the completed product as the chairman's appears to be Dean Burch when chairman of the Federal Communications Commission. Apparently, he remained somewhat aloof from the process. Although he no doubt was consulted in the preparatory stage, he saw the product as a staff responsibility and a reflection of the judgment of the executive director and his staff to be submitted for consideration simultaneously to him and the other commissioners. He defined his role in the process as essentially the same as his colleagues. The budget considered by the commission was not presented as his budget, but as the staff's recommendation, to be considered by all seven on equal footing. This stance seems to be a matter of individual preference on Burch's part, and not a characteristic of the chairmanship in the Federal Communications

Commission. Other chairmen have played a more active role in budget processes.

25. The problem of priorities is discussed in Elman, "Administrative Reform of the Federal Trade Commission," pp. 794–97.

26. See James W. Singer, "Consumer Report/FTC Planning Office Plays Larger Role in Decision Making," *National Journal,* Sept. 13, 1975, p. 1298.

CHAPTER 5.
Organizational Structure and Processes

1. There was, of course, the early initiative to provide for presidential appointment of the Interstate Commerce Commission chairman.

2. There may be other reasons for foregoing large organizational adjustments. A number of chairmen have encountered organizations that had only recently been redone. Others, because of the proximity of their arrival to an upcoming presidential election, realize that their tenure may be of short duration. Still others may simply conclude that existing arrangements are adequate.

3. One reason is the critical importance of their support if there is to be implementation.

4. Civil Aeronautics Board, *Reports to Congress: Fiscal Year 1970* (Washington, D.C.: U.S. Government Printing Office, 1971), p. 70; *Reports to Congress: Fiscal Year 1971* (Washington, D.C.: U.S. Government Printing Office, 1972), p. 78; *Reports to Congress: Fiscal Year 1972* (Washington, D.C.: U.S. Government Printing Office, 1973), pp. 76–77.

5. As have several recent chairmen, for example Dean Burch of the Federal Communications Commission, Lewis Engman of the Federal Trade Commission, and John Robson of the Civil Aeronautics Board.

6. For example, Rosel Hyde, as chairman, introduced the concept of the consent calendar in the Federal Communications Commission, and William Casey instituted changes in Securities and Exchange Commission processes pertaining to decisions on investigations. Lewis Engman, as chairman of the Federal Trade Commission, gave considerable attention to the nature of the information supplied by staff to serve as a basis of decisions and to presentation of alternatives. See Carole Shifrin, "Engman at the FTC: Initiatives Expanded," *Washington Post,* Nov. 30, 1975, p. B13.

7. Charles Murphy, when chairman of the Civil Aeronautics Board, pushed the show-cause concept to expedite modifications of local service carrier certificates and, indeed, roughed out the language for the new procedure. This, according to the board, "has been hailed by administrative lawyers as one of the more significant forward steps in aviation administrative law in at least the last decade." Civil Aeronautics Board, *Reports to Congress: Fiscal Year 1968* (Washington, D.C.: U.S. Government Printing Office, 1969), p. 1.

Setting area natural gas rates through rule-making proceedings, sponsored by John Nassikas while chairman of the Federal Power Commission, is another illustration.

8. Bureau of the Budget, *Management Review of the Federal Trade Commission,* Jan. 1970.

9. The changes are described in, Federal Trade Commission, *Annual Report: Fiscal Year 1970* (Washington, D.C.: U.S. Government Printing Office, 1971), pp. 1–2.

10. Securities and Exchange Commission, *SEC 1972: Thirty-eighth Annual Report* (Washington, D.C.: U.S. Government Printing Office, 1973), pp. 133–35.

11. Office of Management and Budget, *Diagnostic Management Review for the Securities and Exchange Commission,* Sept. 1971, p. II-2.

12. *Ibid.*

13. *Ibid.,* pp. II-4–5.

14. *Ibid.,* p. II-6.

15. *Ibid.,* pp. II-7–9.

16. Securities and Exchange Commission, *SEC 1972,* p. 134.

17. *Ibid.*

18. Office of Management and Budget, *Diagnostic Management Review of the Federal Communications Commission,* July 1972.

19. *Ibid.,* p. III–5.

20. *Ibid.*

21. *Ibid.,* p. IV–5.

22. *Ibid.*

CHAPTER 6.
Chairmen, Commissioners and
Staff Leadership

1. Nicholas Johnson, "The Second Half of Jurisprudence: The Study of Administrative Decision-making," *Stanford Law Review* 23 (Nov. 1970), p. 184.

2. In reference to the Federal Trade Commission in the 1950s, Joseph Palamountain, Jr., observed, "Cases live out their lives beneath the surface, rising to the attention of the Commissioners only a few times. And even then, the normal action is to approve staff recommendations or decisions." "The Administrator's Role—Issues and Hypotheses," paper delivered at the 1961 Annual Meeting of the American Political Science Association, New York, 1960, p. 13. In commenting on the Federal Trade Commission in more recent years, Philip Elman noted, "It is a truism that the law made in litigated administrative cases constitutes but the tip of an iceberg. Much more law is made informally in advisory opinions, for example, or in decisions not to close a particular investigation," suggesting another dimension in staff-commissioner relationships. Indeed, his whole critique is filled with implications regarding the decisional role of the staff. "Administrative Reform of the Federal Trade Commission," p. 785.

3. Civil Aeronautics Board, *Reports to Congress: Fiscal Year 1972.*

4. The distinction between routine and critical decisions is based on that developed by Philip Selznick, *Leadership in Administration,* chap. 2.

5. Carole Shifrin, "FTC Dispute on Gas Reserves Aired," *Washington Post,* June 25, 1975, p. D5.

6. In its early life, the Office of Consumer Advocate played a significant role in increasing carrier liability for lost and damaged luggage, continuing affinity charter flights for a year, and simplifying ticketing regulations. Richard Starnes, "New CAB Unit Is Big on Air Fares," *Knoxville News-Sentinel,* Apr. 28, 1975, p. 28.

7. See, for example, Singer, "Consumer Report/FTC Planning Office Plays Larger Role in Decision Making," p. 1298.

8. Some of the implications are suggested in the discussion of Commissioner Benjamin Hooks' role as backlog commissioner. Subcommittee on Communications, Senate Committee on Commerce, *Hearings, Overview of the Federal Communications Commission,* 93d Cong., 1st sess., 1973, pp. 70–73.

9. Subcommittee on Commerce and Finance, House Committee on Interstate and Foreign Commerce, *Hearings, Securities and Exchange Act Amendments of 1973,* pt. 1, 1973, p. 348.

10. Senate Committee on Commerce, *Hearings, Nominations, June–October,* 93d Cong., 2d sess., 1974, pp. 70–71 and 77–78.

11. There is no evidence to suggest that appointees from within are any less susceptible to the leadership of the chairman than appointees from without.

12. There are exceptions, of course. An interesting example concerns David Schwartz, assistant director of the Federal Power Commission's Office of Economics. Beginning in

late 1973, Schwartz publicly contradicted "official" agency positions on a number of basic energy questions. The differences are discussed in James G. Phillips, "Energy Report/Congress Nears Showdown on Proposal to Decontrol Gas Prices," *National Journal,* May 25, 1974, pp. 769–72.

13. A suggestive example concerns suspended rate matters before the Federal Power Commission. "The staff is . . . in a position to act, to a greater or lesser degree, as a kind of intermediary, or broker between the parties. The extent to which the parties may be swayed by the staff depends, to some extent, upon their estimate of the staff's influence with the commission. On occasion, presumably when the parties were satisfied that the staff spoke for the agency, the staff has been conspicuous in its role of intermediary." Ralph S. Spritzer, "Uses of Summary Power to Suspend Rates: An Examination of Federal Regulatory Agency Practices," *University of Pennsylvania Law Review* 120 (Nov. 1971), p. 91.

14. These comments might be qualified by suggesting that staff may be biased toward activism within the established framework and employing traditional approaches. When activistic chairmen attempt to move outside these boundaries, they may encounter some resistance.

15. The chairman's appointments are considered key indicators. Also, the perceived resistance of chairmen to partisan interests, as in resisting political clearance of appointments and participation in political fund-raising activities, may win plaudits.

16. Senate Committee on Government Operations, *Hearings, Regulatory Reform—1974,* pt. 1, 93d Cong., 2d sess., 1974, p. 94.

17. See Subcommittee on Administrative Practice and Procedure, Senate Committee on the Judiciary, *Hearings, Oversight of Civil Aeronautics Board Practices and Procedures,* vol. 3, 94th Cong., 1st sess., 1975, pp. 2299–469.

18. The Civil Aeronautics Board provides examples of both delay and acceleration. During the early 1970s, reportedly the chief administrative law judge failed to assign four route cases for hearing because of "informal instructions of the chairman's office in connection with the unofficial moratorium on route cases." Jack Egan, "CAB Memo Shows Route Moratorium," *Washington Post,* Feb. 27, 1975, p. F 10. John Robson, who became chairman in 1975, "instructed" the staff to evaluate a proposal for reducing air transportation taxes in relation to increases in the cost of fuel "on an urgent basis." Steve Mott, "CAB Weighs Plan to Cut Taxes as Airline Fuel Costs Increase," *Washington Post,* Sept. 25, 1975, p. C 13.

CHAPTER 7.
Commission Decisions

1. Jack Egan, "CAB Rejects Increase in U.S. Air Fares," *Washington Post,* June 14, 1975, p. D 9.

2. There is a lag of several years in the publication of agency reports. The Interstate Commerce Commission is not discussed because during much of the period for which reported decisions are available, the chairmanship rotated annually among the members.

3. Bradley C. Cannon, "Voting Behavior of the FCC," *Midwest Journal of Political Science* 13 (Nov. 1969), p. 598.

4. Les Brown, "Dissent Held Rare in F.C.C. Voting," *New York Times,* Aug. 12, 1975, p. 59.

5. Chairmen, of course, may lose from time to time on important matters and find themselves dissenting. Toward the end of his time as chairman of the Federal Power Commission, John Nassikas, for example, was in the minority in several very critical natural-gas rate cases.

6. Subcommittee on Reorganization, Research, and International Organization, Senate Committee on Government Operations, *Hearings, S.268, Government in the Sunshine,* 93d Cong., 2d sess., 1974, p. 203.

7. *Ibid.*, p. 235.

8. Johnson and Dystel characterized the role of staff in Federal Communications Commission decision-making in this way: "Those issues which do reach the Commissioners each week often take them by surprise. Opening a new agenda (the stack of mimeographed staff memos and accompanying recommended opinions for a Wednesday meeting) is like Christmas morning. All too often the agenda includes a long, detailed staff document dealing with a controversial and complicated matter in which: (1) numerous alternatives are presented (or excluded) after extensive staff work, (2) the proposed resolution is endorsed by all of the Commission's bureau chiefs, (3) an immediate decision is required, and (4) any alteration in the proposed resolution will mean considerably more staff work and costly delay. As a result, rational decision-making suffers." "A Day in the Life," pp. 1576–77.

9. Subcommittee on Transportation and Aeronautics, House Committee on Interstate and Foreign Commerce, *Hearings, Independent Truckers and the Energy Crisis,* 93d Cong., 2d Sess., 1974, pp. 2–18.

10. Carole Shifrin, "Regulatory Units Hit on Practices," *Washington Post,* Nov. 9, 1974, p. A 9; Jack Eagan, "CAB Rules on Charters Withdrawn," *Washington Post,* Feb. 12, 1975, p. E 1; Morton Mintz, "Probe of Air Fares Delayed," *Washington Post,* Oct. 8, 1975, p. D 9.

11. Chairman John Robson of the Civil Aeronautics Board has made his schedule available to the public. For example, on November 18, 1975, he met with: (1) officials of Eastern Airlines regarding labor, fuel, and other cost problems; (2) Air Transport Association officials regarding their work on regulatory reform; (3) architects on airport design; and (4) officials of Argentine Airlines. Carole Shifrin, "Robson Brings Reform to Troubled CAB," *Washington Post,* Dec. 14, 1975, p. B 17.

12. Further, they may have an impact on the behavior of the regulated, and intentionally so. Secor Browne, when chairman of the Civil Aeronautics Board, commented in a speech to the effect that a bankruptcy among the major airlines would not be a national tragedy, and that the industry should not expect the board to compensate them for inefficiencies. This was a carefully calculated statement aimed at making the carriers more cost conscious. More recently, a chairman of the Interstate Commerce Commission reportedly informally assigned quotas to the various railroads aimed at enlarging the car fleet.

13. The area rate approach was outlined and publicized by Joseph Swidler in a speech prior to its adoption by the Federal Power Commission. As Maisel says in the case of the Federal Reserve Board, "Since the Chairman's views get wide publicity, they may lead to major changes in expectations and, as a result, to changes in actual policy even though they initially reflected a purely personal viewpoint." Maisel, *Managing the Dollar,* p. 125. And those outside the agency may become anxious in the face of silence in the chair. The low profile that Lee White initially maintained as chairman of the Federal Power Commission caused considerable concern in the natural gas and electric power industries, concern subsequently alleviated by a series of speeches and interviews. Gene Smith, "F.P.C.'s White Sees Challenge in Handling Nation's Resources," *New York Times,* Oct. 9, 1966, Sec. 3, p. 1.

14. A recent example occurred with the Washington visitation of a number of independent truckers in 1973. Rising gasoline prices had set off demands for relief and the threat of a massive shutdown of highway transport. Using protest and demonstration politics tactics, the spokesmen for the truckers focused on the government in general and the Interstate Commerce Commission in particular. Engulfed by great public concern and a sense of crisis, the plight of the truckers and their threats, and conflicting and in part seemingly unsound positions being pushed by other government officials, Chairman Stafford of the Interstate Commerce Commission dealt with the protest leaders. In his negotiations with them, statements were made which some of his colleagues considered to be improper commitments made on behalf of the commission without prior consideration. Although the commission did approve the order which translated Stafford's statements into legal reality, at least some commissioners considered the chairman's initiatives in the situation as an unwarranted extension of his prerogatives.

15. Maisel, *Managing the Dollar,* p. 125.

16. There are strategic devices which may be employed to enhance the capacity of chairmen to assert their views. In congressional testimony, for example, comment on sensitive points may be omitted from the prepared statement, with the expectation that the points will be raised in questions, leaving the chairman free to answer as he thinks best. Expression is facilitated by the fact that chairmen generally are not accompanied by other members in appearances before Congress.

17. An interesting example concerns Richard Wiley's reluctance to bring a staff study regarding children's television initiated by his predecessor before the Federal Communications Commission. Subcommittee on Communications, Senate Committee on Commerce, *Hearings, Overview of the Federal Communications Commission,* 93d Cong., 2d sess., 1974, pp. 96–101.

18. On the "children's hour," see John Carmody, "As the Curtain Rises, We See the Network Execs Plotting to . . . ," *Washington Post,* Jan. 19, 1975, p. G 1. See also the letter of November 29, 1974, from Nicholas Johnson, chairman, National Citizens Committee for Broadcasting, to Richard Wiley. Senate Committee on Government Operations, *Hearings, Regulatory Reform—1974,* pt. 2, 1974, pp. 886–87.

An illustration from an earlier period suggests that negotiated understandings, in addition to those on telephone rates, are not just a recent phenomenon. Martin Mayer tells the story:

"The FCC may lack the legal power to influence network programming, but its powers in other areas are so extreme that a few words dropped in the right ears can be remarkably persuasive. Perhaps the most extraordinary example of informal intervention was the call from Chairman John C. Doerfer in 1960 which brought down to the FCC for a little conference the chiefs of all three networks. Doerfer had no rule to propose; indeed, he had not discussed with his fellow Commissioners much of what he was about to say. But he was insistent—and he noted that President Eisenhower agreed with him—that each network must present a public affairs program every week in evening time at an hour when no two such programs would conflict. The network officials had known that something of this sort was in the wind (the FCC is a sieve, one of them says), and they were prepared. The antitrust laws, they said sympathetically, forbade any such collusion among them. Indeed, their lawyers were concerned that they were meeting altogether to discuss programs at all, even under such distinguished auspices as those of Chairman Doerfer. At this point, Doerfer reached into his desk and pulled out a letter from the Attorney General, an official opinion that collaboration among the networks for this purpose would not violate the antitrust laws. Presently, without any Commission action, the networks were following Doerfer's suggestions." "This Means You," *TV Guide,* Nov. 26, 1966, pp. 17–18.

For an illustration drawn from another agency, see Robert J. Samuelson, "Promotional Air Fares to be Banned by CAB," *Washington Post,* Dec. 9, 1972, p. A1.

19. The capacity to influence the agenda may be among the more important resources of Federal Communications Commission chairmen. It has been reported that, "The agenda is the product of industry pressures, staff idiosyncrasies, and political judgments. If he chooses, however, the Chairman is in a position to control the flow of items to the Commission." Johnson and Dystel, "A Day in the Life," p. 1576. For an example of delay aimed at achieving a particular outcome, see Krasnow and Longley, *The Politics of Broadcast Regulation,* pp. 107–108.

20. Maisel, *Managing the Dollar,* p. 126.

21. Other members may request special meetings, but they cannot convene the membership for informal sessions with the same ease as chairmen. As an example of the uses of this capacity, when chairman of the Civil Aeronautics Board Charles Murphy instituted weekly luncheons for the members away from their offices, there was no formal agenda, but there was a chairman's agenda. It was basically during these sessions that he briefed the members

regarding activities in the chairman's office, consulted with them, and secured their agreement on matters for which he wished their support. In addition, the discussions laid groundwork for decisions to be made later in formal sessions. Beyond the particulars, the meetings were intended to stimulate a sense of participation on the part of the members in all aspects of the board's work and a sense of collegiality.

22. The potential ironies here are suggested by a member who served with a chairman who opened commission-level decision-making processes to staff in a generous fashion and who seemingly viewed staff presence as helpful in terms of his interests. In the view of the member, his own influence on decisions was greater when staff was present than when it was absent. Under more open circumstances, it was difficult for the chairman to hold to a position that was "unreasonable." The same might be said for other members, also. In general there are indications that the more open the processes of choice to the staff, the better the decisions in terms of clarity, the articulation of the bases for choice, and the like. Closed processes provide more opportunity for negotiated outcomes, or, as one put it, "wheeling and dealing" on the part of members.

23. Maisel, *Managing the Dollar,* p. 127.

24. *Ibid.*

25. Cary, *Politics and the Regulatory Agencies,* pp. 84–85.

26. Redford, *The Regulatory Process,* p. 303.

27. Cary, *Politics and the Regulatory Agencies,* chap. 4.

28. Krasnow and Longley, *The Politics of Broadcast Regulation,* pp. 1–3. See also Robert J. Samuelson, "Name-Calling at the FCC," *Washington Post,* Feb. 18, 1972, p. C1.

29. Max Frankel, *New York Times,* Jan. 8, 1968, p. 52. Quoted in Lawrence C. Pierce, *The Politics of Fiscal Policy Formation* (Pacific Palisades, Calif.: Goodyear Publishing Co., 1971), p. 99.

30. For an illustration concerning E. William Henry and the Federal Communication Commission's proposed CATV rules of 1966, see Krasnow and Longley, *The Politics of Broadcast Regulation,* p. 30.

31. As an example, note the FCC's reversal regarding domestic communication satellites, which resulted from a major effort on the part of Dean Burch.

32. Simon Lazarus, *The Genteel Populists* (New York: Holt, 1974), p. 106.

33. William Cary mentions such incentives. *Politics and the Regulatory Agencies,* pp. 10–11.

34. Some chairmen may see the preoccupation of members with such tasks as a means for enlarging their influence in another sense. While their colleagues are out about the country or the world, the chairman is at the office running the agency and steeping himself in the matters to be decided.

35. In some instances, chairmen have gone beyond consultation and given members special assignments in connection with major agency undertakings. This does not happen with great frequency, however.

36. Cary, *Politics and the Regulatory Agencies,* p. 10.

37. Cary mentions a fellow chairman as an example. *Ibid.*

38. This is true for the Federal Communications Commission as well as for the Interstate Commerce Commission in connection with one chairman who served during the 1960s. This ICC chairman, reputed to have been influential in some reappointment decisions, is still recalled with disfavor by some, because he is perceived to have compromised the political independence of the agency by such involvements.

39. This view was generally shared by those interviewed. With specific reference to the Federal Communications Commission, former commissioner Kenneth Cox has said that a chairman "definitely has some edge in influence." Further, "there is some inclination on the part of some individual commissioners, if they don't feel strongly about a matter, to go along with the Chairman if he wants to say something is a matter of importance to him."

"What It's Like Inside the FCC," *Telephony,* Sept. 5, 1970, pp. 56–57. Quoted in Krasnow and Longley, *The Politics of Broadcast Regulation,* p. 30.

40. This goes somewhat against the themes developed in much of the small group litera-ture. But it is somewhat compatible with Sidney Ulmer's conclusions about judicial decision-making. He has said: "A formally designated leader in a collegial court influences the behavior of his group not by virtue of his administrative effectiveness or congenial air, not because his colleagues decide he deserves to be followed, but simply because his position carries with it power that can be used effectively to determine certain kinds of issues. This is a direct conse-quence of group structure and rules of procedure within a structure." Ulmer, *Courts as Small and Not Small Groups,* p. 21.

41. A member who served under two chairmen with vastly different styles commented on this point. He said, in effect, that he liked the congenial, colleague-oriented chairman better. But it was a better commission under the chairman who was aggressive and who was inclined to go on his own to a much greater extent. The basis for the judgment was the nature and quality of the decisions that were made under the two regimes.

42. Sidney Verba, *Small Groups and Political Behavior,* p. 200.

43. Paul Rand Dixon's difficulties with his colleagues have been discussed at several points. Two chairmen of the Federal Maritime Commission, William Harllee and Helen Delich Bentley, had difficulties also, although the conflicts on the surface seemed over trifles, involving such things as access to the agency's automobiles. Toward the end of his tenure as chairman of the Federal Power Commission, the relationship between Joseph Swidler and his colleagues came under severe strain. The immediate cause was the preparation of a report at the request of the White House on the Northeast Blackout. Swidler saw the task as essentially the responsibility of the chairman and resisted the participation of his colleagues. They saw large policy implications in the report and insisted on involvement. The feeling developed on the part of some that they were being excluded from matters in which they had large respon-sibilities. As a result, resentment evolved. This took place when it was known that Swidler would not be reappointed as chairman and shortly before he left office. In fact, the blackout caused him to delay his announced departure. Thus the effects of the disagreement did not have an opportunity to play themselves out in the work of the agency.

CHAPTER 8.
Regulatory Agency Governance: Summing up

1. A comprehensive discussion of agency reorganization efforts is contained in "The Progress of Federal Agency Reorganization Under the Kennedy Administration," *Virginia Law Review,* 48 (Mar. 1962), p. 300.

2. In Sept. 1976 the Government in the Sunshine Act became law. Henceforward, the business of the seven agencies, as well as many others, must be conducted in public sessions with limited exceptions. Unquestionably, the law will have a major impact on commission meetings and the environment in which decisions in proceedings will be made. The nature of that impact is difficult to predict. It does not seem, however, that agency governance and especially the chairman's place in it will be altered in basic respects. The major reason is that much that chairmen do is outside formal commission gatherings. Indeed, the chairman's place may be strengthened as a result of a reluctance to bring into the sunshine certain matters previously discussed collectively, leaving them instead for the chairman to handle.

3. See the discussion in chap. 1, p. 4 *et seq.*

4. The President's Advisory Council on Executive Organization, *A New Regulatory Framework,* p. 33.

5. Bernstein, *Regulating Business by Independent Commission,* p. 173.

6. See n. 8, chap. 1.

7. Louis M. Kohlmeier, "Big Government a Campaign Issue," *National Journal,* Nov. 1, 1975, p. 1520.

8. *Ibid.*

9. Senator William Brock recently asked former Federal Trade Commission chairman Miles W. Kirkpatrick whether "the Commission has a life of its own?" Kirkpatrick's response suggested the subtle resonance of chairmen and administrations. "I believe that what you say may be something of a surface reaction. I think you will find when there is a change of guard, in some instance, at least, the kind of activity and its direction may well change." Senate Committee on Government Operations, *Hearings, Regulatory Reform—1974,* pt. 1, 1974, p. 53.

10. Reported examples include solicitation of staff members in the Federal Trade Commission while Paul Rand Dixon was chairman and solicitation from firms by Federal Maritime Commission chairman Helen Delich Bentley. See Elman, "Administrative Reform of the Federal Trade Commission," p. 855; and Jack Anderson's column in the *Washington Post,* Nov. 30, 1973, p. D21.

11. See, for example, Aaron Wildavsky, *Dixon-Yates: A Study in Power Politics* (New Haven: Yale Univ. Press, 1962), chap. 11.

12. The delicate handling of Securities and Exchange Commission materials concerning Robert Vescoe by William Casey when those materials were of interest to a Democratic-controlled congressional committee is an illustration. Special Subcommittee on Investigations, House Interstate and Foreign Commerce Committee, *Hearings, Legislative Oversight of the SEC: Agency Independence and the ITT Case,* 93d Cong., 1st sess., 1973.

13. Mark V. Nadel has suggested that agencies within the executive branch are more susceptible to use for purposes of paying political debts than the independent agencies. Nadel, *The Politics of Consumer Protection,* p. 97.

14. The previously noted conflict between the Consumer Product Safety Commission and the Civil Service Commission regarding White House clearance of appointees to NEA positions revealed some concerns. They are also expressed at various points in Subcommittee on Commerce and Finance, House Interstate and Foreign Commerce Committee, *Hearings, Securities and Exchange Act Amendments of 1973,* pt. 1, 1973.

15. Quoted in Bruce E. Thorp, "Agency Report/Office of Telecommunications Policy Speaks for President—and Hears Some Static," *National Journal,* Feb. 13, 1971, p. 345.

16. Richard P. Nathan, *The Plot that Failed: Nixon and the Administrative Presidency* (New York: John Wiley and Sons, 1975), p. 40.

17. See Linda E. Demkovich, "Transportation Report/ICC Resists Ford Moves to Cut Its Power Over Rails," *National Journal,* July 5, 1975, p. 993.

18. The Federal Trade Commission was recently successful in clarifying its relationship with the Department of Justice and enlarging its information-gathering capacities despite presidential opposition. Jack Gardner, Richard Corrigan, and Joel Havemann, "Energy Report/Presidential Veto of Pipeline Bill Threatened Despite Fuel Shortage," *National Journal,* Nov. 10, 1973, p. 1693.

19. Richard E. Cohen, "Regulatory Report 11/Lack of Consensus Precludes Major, Speedy 'Reform'," *National Journal,* May 17, 1975, p. 723.

20. Two recent instances in which performance was clearly a factor in the replacement of chairmen concerned Robert Timm of the Civil Aeronautics Board and John Powell of the Equal Employment Opportunity Commission. See Louis M. Kohlmeier, "Aborting the Trip of Chairman Timm," *National Journal,* Nov. 23, 1974, p. 1777; and James W. Singer, "Employment Report/Forced Resignations Allow Revamping of EEOC," *National Journal,* Mar. 22, 1975, p. 447.

21. Senate Committee on Government Operations, *Hearings, Regulatory Reform—1974,* pt. 2, 1974, p. 868.

22. Lyndon B. Johnson often was cited in the interviews as a president who established

a clear hands-off stance regarding particular regulatory determinations.

23. Richard E. Cohen, "Regulatory Report/White House Task Force Turns Its Sights toward Congress," *National Journal*, Nov. 22, 1975, pp. 1604–45.

24. Subcommittee on Commerce and Finance, House Committee on Interstate and Foreign Commerce, *Hearings, Securities and Exchange Act Amendments of 1973*, pt. 1, 1973, p. 248.

Selected Bibliography:
Regulatory Policy and Administration

Anderson, James E. *Emergence of the Modern Regulatory State.* Washington, D.C.: Public Affairs Press, 1962.

——, ed. *Economic Regulatory Policies.* Lexington, Mass.: Lexington, 1976.

Bernstein, Marver H. *Regulating Business by Independent Commission.* Princeton: Princeton Univ. Press, 1955.

——. "The Regulatory Process: A Framework for Analysis," *Law and Contemporary Problems* 26 (Spring 1961), pp. 329–46.

——. "Independent Regulatory Agencies: A Perspective on Their Reform," *The Annals of the American Academy of Political and Social Science* 400 (Mar. 1972), pp. 14–26.

Bock, Edwin A., ed. *Government Regulation of Business: A Casebook.* Englewood Cliffs, N.J.: Prentice-Hall, 1965.

Breyer, Stephen G., and Paul W. MacAvoy. *Energy Regulation by the Federal Power Commission.* Washington, D.C.: The Brookings Institution, 1974.

Brown, Keith C. *Regulation of the Natural Gas Producing Industry.* Washington, D.C.: Resources for the Future, Inc., 1972.

Cannon, Bradley C. "Voting Behavior on the FCC," *Midwest Journal of Political Science* 13 (Nov. 1969), pp. 587–612.

Capron, William M., ed. *Technological Change in Regulated Industries.* Washington, D.C.: The Brookings Institution, 1971.

Cary, William L. *Politics and the Regulatory Agencies.* New York: McGraw-Hill, 1967.

Caves, Richard E. *Air Transport and Its Regulators.* Cambridge, Mass.: Harvard Univ. Press, 1962.

Cox, Edward F., Robert G. Fellmeth, and John E. Schulz. *"The Nader Report" on the Federal Trade Commission.* New York: Richard W. Baron, 1969.

Cramton, Roger C. "Regulatory Structure and Regulatory Performance: A Critique of the Ash Council Report," *Public Administration Review* 32 (July/ Aug. 1972), pp. 284–91.

Cushman, Robert E. *The Independent Regulatory Commissions.* New York: Oxford Univ. Press, 1941.

Cutler, Lloyd N., and David R. Johnson. "Regulation and the Political Process," *The Yale Law Journal* 84 (June 1975), pp. 1395–1418.

Douglas, George W., and James C. Miller III. *Economic Regulation of Domestic Air Transport.* Washington, D.C.: The Brookings Institution, 1974.

Edelman, Murray. *The Symbolic Uses of Politics.* Urbana, Ill.: Univ. of Illinois Press, 1964.

Elman, Philip. "Administration Reform of the Federal Trade Commission," *The Georgetown Law Journal* 59 (Mar. 1971), pp. 777–860.

Fainsod, Merle. "Some Reflections on the Nature of the Regulatory Process." In Carl J. Friedrich and Edward S. Mason, eds., *Public Policy,* vol. I. Cambridge, Mass.: Harvard Univ. Press, 1940, chap. 10.

Fellmeth, Robert. *The Interstate Commerce Omission.* New York: Grossman, 1970.

Friendly, Henry J. *The Federal Administrative Agencies: The Need for Better Definition of Standards.* Cambridge, Mass.: Harvard Univ. Press, 1962.

Fritschler, A. Lee. *Smoking and Politics: Policymaking and the Federal Bureaucracy.* New York: Appleton, 1969.

Gellhorn, Ernest. "Adverse Publicity by Administrative Agencies," *Harvard Law Review* 86 (June 1973), pp. 1380–1441.

Graham, George A., and Henry Reining, Jr., eds. *Regulatory Administration.* New York: Wiley, 1943.

Hall, Hugh M., Jr. "Responsibility of President and Congress for Regulatory Policy Development," *Law and Contemporary Problems* 26 (Spring 1961), pp. 261–81.

Heady, Ferrel. "The New Reform Movement in Regulatory Administration," *Public Administration Review* 19 (Spring 1959), pp. 89–100.

Hector, Louis J. "Problems of the CAB and the Independent Regulatory Commissions," *The Yale Law Journal* 69 (May 1960), pp. 931–64.

Herring, E. Pendleton. *Public Administration and the Public Interest.* New York: McGraw-Hill, 1936.

———. *Federal Commissioners: A Study of Their Careers and Qualifications.* Cambridge, Mass.: Harvard Univ. Press, 1936.

Huntington, Samuel P. "The Marasmus of the ICC: The Commission, the Railroads, and the Public Interest," *The Yale Law Journal* 61 (Apr. 1952), pp. 467–509.

Hyneman, Charles S. *Bureaucracy in a Democracy.* New York: Harper and Row, 1950.

Jaffe, Louis L. "The Effective Limits of the Administrative Process: A Reevaluation," *Harvard Law Review* 67 (May 1954), pp. 1105–35.

———. "The Illusion of the Ideal Administration," *Harvard Law Review* 86 (May 1973), pp. 1183–99.

Johnson, Nicholas. "A New Fidelity to the Regulatory Ideal," *The Georgetown Law Journal* 59 (Mar. 1971), pp. 869–908.

———, and John Jay Dystel. "A Day in the Life: The Federal Communications Commission," *The Yale Law Journal* 82 (July 1973), pp. 1575–1634.

Kohlmeier, Louis M., Jr. *The Regulators: Watchdog Agencies and the Public Interest.* New York: Harper, 1969.

Krasnow, Erwin G., and Lawrence D. Longley. *The Politics of Broadcast Regulation.* New York: St. Martins, 1973.

Landis, James M. *The Administrative Process.* New Haven: Yale Univ. Press, 1938.
——. *Report on Regulatory Agencies to the President-elect.* Washington, D.C.: U.S. Senate Judiciary Committee, 86th Cong., 2d sess., 1960. Committee Print.
Latham, Earl. *The Politics of Railroad Coordination: 1933-1936.* Cambridge, Mass.: Harvard Univ. Press, 1959.
Lawrence, Samuel A. *United States Merchant Shipping Policies and Politics.* Washington, D.C.: The Brookings Institution, 1966.
Leiserson, Avery. *Administrative Regulation: A Study in Representation of Interests.* Chicago: Univ. of Chicago Press, 1942.
Lowi, Theodore J. *The End of Liberalism.* New York: Norton, 1969.
MacAvoy, Paul W., ed. *The Crisis of the Regulatory Commissions.* New York: Norton, 1970.
McConnell, Grant. *Private Power and American Democracy.* New York: Knopf, 1966.
Maisel, Sherman J. *Managing the Dollar.* New York: Norton, 1973.
Morgan, Charles S. "A Critique of 'The Marasmus of the ICC: The Commission, the Railroads and the Public Interest,'" *The Yale Law Journal* 62 (Jan. 1953), pp. 171-225.
Nadel, Mark V. *The Politics of Consumer Protection.* Indianapolis: Bobbs-Merrill, 1971.
Nagel, Stuart, and Martin Lubin. "Regulatory Commissioners and Party Politics," *Administrative Law Review* 17 (Fall 1964), pp. 39-47.
Noll, Roger G. *Reforming Regulation: An Evaluation of the Ash Council Proposals.* Washington, D.C.: The Brookings Institution, 1971.
——, Merton J. Peck, and John J. McGowan. *Economic Aspects of Television Regulation.* Washington, D.C.: The Brookings Institution, 1973.
Phillips, Almarin, ed. *Promoting Competition in Regulated Markets.* Washington, D.C.: The Brookings Institution, 1975.
Porter, Michael E., and Jeffrey F. Sagansky. "Information, Politics, and Economic Analysis: The Regulatory Decision Process in the Air Freight Case," *Public Policy* 24 (Spring 1976), pp. 263-307.
Posner, Richard A. "Theories of Economic Regulation," *The Bell Journal of Economics and Management Science* 5 (Autumn 1974), pp. 335-58.
"The Progress of Federal Agency Reorganization Under the Kennedy Administration," *Virginia Law Review* 48 (Mar. 1962), pp. 300-77.
Reagan, Michael D. "The Political Structure of the Federal Reserve System," *American Political Science Review* 55 (Mar. 1961), pp. 64-76.
Redford, Emmette S. *Administration of National Economic Control.* New York: Macmillan, 1952.
——. *American Government and the Economy.* New York: Macmillan, 1965.
——. "The President and the Regulatory Commissions," *Texas Law Review* 44 (Dec. 1965), p. 288.
——. *The Regulatory Process: With Illustrations from Commercial Aviation.* Austin: Univ. of Texas Press, 1969.
Robinson, Glen O. "On Reorganizing the Independent Regulatory Agencies," *Virginia Law Review* 57 (Sept. 1971), pp. 947-95.

———, and Ernest Gellhorn. *The Administrative Process.* St. Paul, Minn.: West, 1974.

Rosenblum, Victor G. "How to Get into TV: The Federal Communications Commission and Miami's Channel 10," in Alan F. Westin, ed., *The Uses of Power: 7 Cases in American Politics.* New York: Harcourt, 1962, chap. 4.

Scher, Seymour. "Congressional Committee Members as Independent Agency Overseers: A Case Study," *American Political Science Review* 54 (Dec. 1960), pp. 911–20.

———. "Regulatory Agency Control Through Appointment: The Case of the Eisenhower Administration and the NLRB," *Journal of Politics* 23 (Nov. 1961), pp. 667–88.

———. "The Politics of Agency Organization," *Western Political Quarterly* 15 (June 1962), pp. 328–44.

Seidman, Harold. *Politics, Position, and Power.* New York: Oxford Univ. Press, 1970.

Shapiro, Martin. *The Supreme Court and Administrative Agencies.* New York: Free Press, 1968.

Stanley, David T., Dean E. Mann, and Jameson W. Doig. *Men Who Govern: A Biographical Profile of Federal Political Executives.* Washington, D.C.: The Brookings Institution, 1967.

Stewart, Richard B. "The Reformation of American Administrative Law," *Harvard Law Review* 88 (June 1975), pp. 1667–1813.

Stigler, George J. *The Citizen and the State: Essays on Regulation.* Chicago: Univ. of Chicago Press, 1975.

Stone, Alan. "The F.T.C. and Advertising Regulation: An Examination of Agency Failure," *Public Policy* 21 (Spring 1973), pp. 203–34.

Tanenhaus, Joseph. "Supreme Court Attitudes Toward Federal Administrative Agencies," *Journal of Politics* 22 (August 1960), pp. 502–24.

Thomas, Norman C. "Politics, Structure and Personnel in Administrative Regulation," *Virginia Law Review* 57 (Sept. 1971), pp. 1033–68.

U.S. Commission on Organization of the Executive Branch of the Government. *Task Force Report on Regulatory Commissions.* Washington, D.C.: U.S. Government Printing Office, 1949.

———. *The Independent Regulatory Commissions,* Report No. 12. Washington, D.C.: U.S. Government Printing Office, 1949.

U.S. President's Advisory Council on Executive Organization. *A New Regulatory Framework: Report on Selected Independent Regulatory Agencies.* Washington, D.C.: U.S. Government Printing Office, 1971.

U.S. President's Committee on Administrative Management. *Report of the Committee with Studies of Administrative Management in the Federal Government.* Washington, D.C.: U.S. Government Printing Office, 1937.

U.S. Senate Committee on Commerce. *Appointments to the Regulatory Agencies: The Federal Communications Commission and the Federal Trade Commission (1949–1974).* Washington, D.C.: U.S. Government Printing Office, 1976. Study prepared by James M. Graham and Victor H. Kramer.

Welborn, David M. "Presidents, Regulatory Commissioners and Regulatory Policy," *Journal of Public Law* 15, no. 1 (1966), pp. 3–29.

———. "Assigning Responsibility for Regulatory Decisions to Individual Commissioners: The Case of the ICC," *Administrative Law Review* 18 (Winter–Spring 1966), pp. 13–28.

Wildavsky, Aaron. *Dixon-Yates: A Study in Power Politics.* New Haven: Yale Univ. Press, 1962.

Wilson, James Q. "The Dead Hand of Regulation," *The Public Interest,* no. 25 (Fall 1971), pp. 39–58.

———. "The Politics of Regulation." In James W. McKie, ed., *Social Responsibility and the Business Predicament.* Washington, D.C.: The Brookings Institution, 1974, chap. 6.

Woll, Peter. *Administrative Law: The Informal Process.* Berkeley and Los Angeles: Univ. of California Press, 1963.

Index